Growing Through Grief

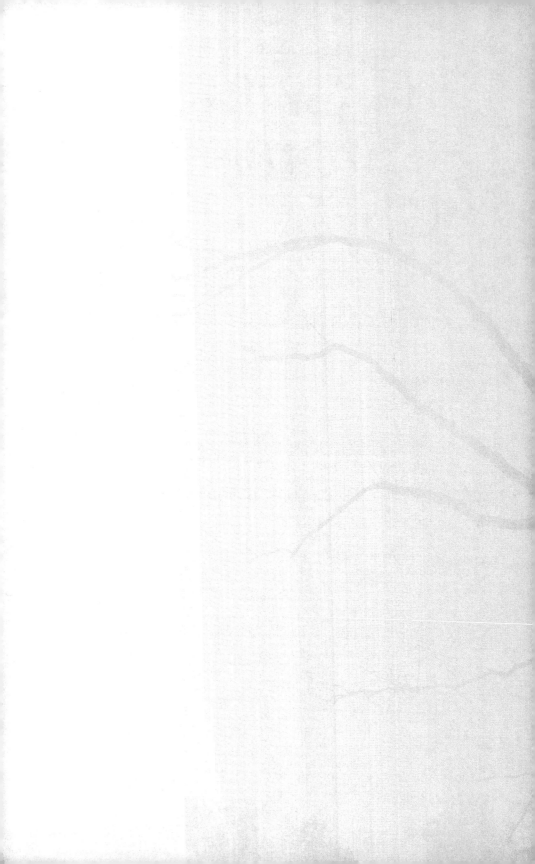

Growing Through Grief

Jenny Landon

A guide to healthy healing
after losing a loved one
to suicide

GROWING OUT OF DARKNESS™
G·O·O·D

Start now. Start where you are.
Start with fear. Start with pain.
Start with doubt.
Start with hands shaking.
Start with voice trembling but start.
Start and don't stop.
Start where you are,
With what you have.
Just . . . Start.

—Ijeoma Umebinyuo

Published by Growing Out Of Darkness

ISBN: 978-0-578-19787-6

Printed in the United States of America

Book Design by Christopher Fayers
Cover photograph taken by Kaeli Landon (age 10)

Table of Contents

When there's a fresh wound in your heart,
keep it open until it heals. Air it out.
Understand it. Dive into it. Be fierce enough to
become it. If you ignore it, it won't be able to
breathe. If you ignore it, it will merely deepen,
spread and resurface later, wanting to release.
And when later happens, it will hurt even
more, because you won't know what you're
bleeding for. Remain with it until it clears, and
watch the beauty pour into your openness.
Remain open to feel lightness. Remain open to
feel free.

—Victoria Erickson

The Author

As the founder of Growing Out Of Darkness (GOOD) and a survivor of suicide, Jenny Landon has taken the most traumatic experience of her life and turned it into a passion for helping others. Jenny's journey began in 1999 after the loss of her father. Determined to understand his death, she focused the remainder of her undergraduate studies on depression and how to heal after experiencing such a loss. Jenny has channeled the benefits of several means of therapy to truly heal her mind and her soul while leading a life focused on helping others to do the same.

www.growingoutofdarkness.org

Foreword

When someone loses a family member to suicide they are never the same again. Often, the resulting trauma substantially stunts or even stops emotional and spiritual growth, sometimes for years, as individuals struggle to recalibrate to a new life without their loved one. Jenny authentically shares her heart-wrenching journey of loss and painful personal growth, weaving it into a beautiful package of immense hope for those recovering from a loved one's suicide. By sharing tools for healthy grieving, communication, and spiritual renewal, Jenny offers a welcome hand back into the fullness of life.

As a therapist I'm always searching for fantastic resources to offer clients and friends and I won't hesitate to recommend her book to those needing reassurance, hope, and new tools for communication and renewed spirituality in the aftermath of suicide.

Tracy Goza, PhD, LPC,
Author of *I Heart Heaven*

The soul always knows what to do to heal itself. The challenge is to silence the mind.

—Caroline Myss

Introduction

My desire to create a guide to healthy healing comes from a place of love, and an overwhelming urge to offer support to those who need it most. It has now been seventeen years since I lost my dad to suicide, and for the last two and a half years, I have been on an incredible journey that has helped me to gain even more perspective into the devastating effects of depression and suicide, while also witnessing sincere love and support shared between those touched by it.

My journey began with documenting my own loss and the steps I took to find balance and happiness. However, it became so much more as I continued to attend support groups in an effort to be certain that this guide to healthy healing includes common aspects of grief experienced by most, if not all, survivors of suicide.

Taking on the task of collecting and effectively communicating the experiences, which I have been exposed to, has been a time consuming process . . . one I didn't want to rush. It was important to me that I share my healing process in a way that was both respectful and vulnerable with the hope of truly connecting with each reader. I tried to share personal information in each chapter in an effort to personalize the material with the hope that it would resonate on a deeper level. One chapter in particular was a struggle due to the fact that I was relying on my siblings to collaborate with me in order to demonstrate my message.

Nearly three years after starting this book, I feel that it is important to share that my biggest delay in completing this guide was brought on by self-doubt. I questioned if I could really be of help to others. And to be completely honest, I was scared to put myself out there.

In the spring of 2016, I was at a retreat where I shared how the impact of my dad's suicide had helped me to become the person I am today. One of the women attending later approached me at a time when we could speak privately. She began by telling me that, while I was sharing my story, she couldn't help but think of the following quote, "Don't judge people before you truly know them. The truth may surprise you."

She shared with me that she had always thought of that quote as a message to encourage people to not make snap judgments upon meeting someone who may have made a negative first impression. It wasn't until hearing me speak about my loss that she realized that it also applies to people who seem to have it all. Until now she had only seen me as a happy young lady living a full life. She never imagined that I had experienced such a loss. She thanked me for having the courage to speak so openly about my struggles and the steps I have taken to heal. She went on to tell me about her own experiences and helped me to realize that my ability to speak openly about my journey has the potential to help others do the same.

It is now my turn to thank her for being the motivation I needed to see this project through.

Similar to the lotus we all possess the ability to grow through the darkness transforming our surroundings into a place of peace.

—Jenny Landon

April 29, 2016 —
Suicide Sucks

Minneapolis, MN

After what had been a week of gray, rainy, cold days, it felt amazing to feel the sun shine again. It should have been a day to rejoice, to be outside listening to the children play on the nearby playground; and yet I found myself sitting in a chapel staring down at a picture of what appeared to be a happy man. I couldn't help but look at his picture and feel the pain his family must be feeling as we prepared to say our final goodbyes to him.

He was a son, a friend, a husband, and a father. He was 38 years old—too young to say goodbye. As I waited for the service to commence, I was overwhelmed by the memories of losing my dad. I was suddenly reminded of the all-consuming, intense, and raw pain of feeling like my heart had been ripped from my chest, and that I might not ever fully be able to catch my breath again.

My eyes filled with tears as I watched this man's wife prepare to say goodbye. I watched their oldest daughter, who at age 19, was only one year younger than I was when I lost my dad. I watched their two young daughters play with their friends; too young to fully understand the gravity of all that was happening around them, and for that I was grateful.

The service began; with his mother standing next to his father, his father spoke of him. He spoke of the son he raised. His pride and love for the man his son grew into was evident in all he shared. His pain intensified as he described losing his son too soon.

His best friend approached the podium to speak. He made us laugh with his commentary describing their friendship, and he brought us to tears as he spoke about his best friend being there for him when he lost his wife only three years prior also to suicide.

His words were powerful and shocking. By speaking so openly about suicide, he gave everyone permission to be real about how we lost this man. He spoke of all the pain suicide causes, and all the joy it robs us of experiencing. Throughout his message he would say, "Suicide sucks," and then continue telling us more about how it had impacted his life, and the impact it can have on everyone it touches.

His message was well prepared and beautiful. What I took away, as the most important thing he wanted us to remember, was that suicide isn't who his friend was. His friend was an amazing son, friend, husband, and father. Suicide stole him from us.

Suicide sucks!

Healing is not an overnight process. It is a daily cleansing of pain, it is a daily healing of your life.

—Leon Brown

Growing Through Grief

I was 20 years old when I lost my dad to suicide. It was a day that would forever change my life. I was a daddy's girl who looked to him for advice, support, approval, and above all else, love. His death nearly shattered my world. The initial pain was almost unbearable, but years later I would realize that his death saved my life.

For those of you who are fairly new to the grieving process, or maybe you're not so new but you're still feeling consumed by the pain, it might be hard to understand how I can perceive my dad's death as a blessing. It's not that I don't miss him, it's not that I don't still have sad moments, and it's absolutely not that I'm happy about his death. My ability to see his death as a blessing has come from working through the hardships involved, and recognizing all that I have learned and gained by going through this loss.

Over the years, I have been exposed to various methods of healing as well as had the opportunity to be influenced by some truly remarkable people. Sadly, I have also attended counseling sessions and support groups that I felt were detrimental; especially to those around me who had not been exposed to the same type of healthy healing opportunities I had experienced. It was this realization that first urged me to start identifying what had helped me the most and to share it with others.

My hope is that through sharing my experiences with you, you, too, can fully grow through your own grief and eventually find peace within yourself and with your loss. Please know you are not alone in your grief and it is possible to feel happiness after experiencing such a loss.

Two realities each person must come to terms with to achieve healthy healing after experiencing the loss of a loved one:

1. There is not a *healthy* quick and easy fix when it comes to grief. It is possible to dull the pain through medication, drugs/alcohol, and denial. But for you to achieve true healing and return to a state of happiness, you must first experience the pain. You must go through the struggles and allow yourself to feel the rawness that comes from such a loss in order to become stronger and more grounded in your ability to move forward and live a healthy and happy life. Once you've done this, you'll be able to look back on this difficult situation and recognize the good that can come from such a tragedy.

2. Time does *not* heal all wounds. It is not the passing of time that heals your pain; it is what you do during that time that will determine not only how "quickly" you heal, but more importantly how healthy you're healing experience will be.

I'm better off healed than I ever was unbroken.

—Beth Moore

Coping after Losing a Loved One to Suicide

Losing a loved one to suicide is a traumatic experience which takes its toll on those left behind. It can cause physical, emotional, and spiritual pain. It is important to be aware of your own wellbeing and to find healthy ways to deal with the pain caused by this loss.

"Survivor of suicide" is a common term referring to someone who lost a loved one to suicide. I highly recommend finding a Survivors of Suicide support group to participate in. Many people who have lost a loved one to suicide have found comfort in being around others who can relate to their pain. Most Survivors of Suicide support groups provide a safe place to openly discuss the loss and the emotional upheaval that comes from such an experience.

During the first few months following my dad's death, I felt as though I was in a fog when anyone would ask me how I was doing. After the shock wore off, I found myself feeling guilty whenever I sensed I was making someone feel uncomfortable by talking openly about him or his suicide. Conversations involving my dad had become awkward. I didn't know how to act, and I never wanted anyone to feel sorry for me or feel obligated to comfort me.

Attending survivors of suicide support groups provided me with a sense of safety. During these meetings, I didn't have to worry about making anyone feel uncomfortable. I was free to talk about my dad, how he died, and how I felt about everything. There was no need to worry about the uncomfortable silence that often occurred while talking to a friend. It was a place where I knew I could go to unload my thoughts and feelings. Support groups also provided me the opportunity to talk about my dad without having to worry about the awkward transition that comes when talking to friends and family about something so heavy but realizing the need to move on to lighter topics. At the end of the session I could return to my normal life talking about anything other than my dad.

Though I have an appreciation for support groups, I have become aware that there seems to be an unspoken ranking for who feels the most pain after losing someone to suicide. There is a sense that a person who has lost a child endures the greatest level of pain, followed by the loss of a spouse, then the loss of a sibling or parent, followed by the loss of a friend. There is rarely any discussion of the pain felt by those who were "mere acquaintances."

While I believe the intensity of pain felt is impacted by the type of relationship one had with the individual who was lost to suicide, I don't believe any one person's grief is more **real** than another person's. Yet during almost every meeting I've attended, one survivor will say to another something to the effect of *I know my pain isn't anything compared to yours.*

It is hard to know exactly how many people are affected by the loss of just one person to suicide. I will never forget being at the funeral home for my dad's service. The building was over-flowing with people who had come to pay their respect. Each person had somehow known my dad; regardless of how well they knew him, each one of them had been touched by his suicide. Each one of them, along with all of those who were unable to attend his funeral, is a survivor of suicide.

Regardless of how well you knew the person who died, or how close of a relationship you had with them, suicide is shocking and heartbreaking. It causes people to question the world around them. For some, the grief is debilitating. For others, the pain might not be as intense, but still resonates on a level in which support from others could be beneficial.

Support groups are intended for people to support one another. No one should feel the need to justify the grief they're experiencing. Nor should they avoid seeking help because they believe they don't have the right to feel such grief. Each one of us has our own struggles to face and our own journey to healthy healing. While I would encourage all survivors of suicide to participate in a support group, I would advise you to attend these meetings alone. It can be challenging for two people who've lost the same person to fully open up and process their grief.

Below is a list of websites that offer information regarding support for Survivors of Suicide. If you discover that there isn't a local support group near you, there are online options.

www.suicide.org
www.afsp.org
www.allianceofhope.org
www.save.org

It is important to note that online options can offer support and a sense of community. However, they can also cause people to fall deeper into their grief sometimes preventing them from moving forward. I have heard from some survivors of suicide that they didn't find comfort from the online forums because of the amount of negativity and anger that some people shared with the group. While additional survivors described their healing process as being stunted due to feeling consumed with the need to be online interacting with others who could relate and understand their pain.

Some survivors have discussed the danger of getting caught up in a vicious cycle which often involves the need to continuously publish posts that will illicit numerous supportive responses. The survivor will feel the lows of grief with each post they publish in order to feel the highs from the responses which often reflect a sense of compassion, understanding, and support.

It is also easy to get caught up and emotionally invested in the losses of other people. The raw emotion posted by others will often resonate and stir up new and old emotions regarding your own loss. It is vital to our healing process that we have a balance between feeling comforted in knowing we are not alone in our loss and protecting ourselves from spending too much time and energy in a space filled with grief.

I highly recommend that you establish healthy boundaries when using any of the online forums. It is good to set parameters that include how often you access the online options as well as how much time you spend on them.

In addition to support groups and traditional counseling, I'm also an advocate for alternative and holistic remedies. Following my dad's death, I began having panic attacks on a regular basis. I was fortunate to have a friend who introduced me to acupuncture. The acupuncture not only alleviated my panic attacks, it also helped me to feel an overall sense of calm and peace unlike anything I had ever experienced. Acupuncture was not a quick fix; it required regular weekly appointments. However, within a few weeks, I started feeling the benefits. I truly believe it was a vital element to my healing.

Recently I was speaking to my acupuncturist about the benefits of choosing acupuncture over Western medication. He shared with me what I believe to be the best illustration to help people have a better perspective of the long term benefits of acupuncture and other alternative healing options.

Your child comes home from school one day with a rather difficult homework assignment. As the parent, you have two choices on how to help your child get through the evening:

1. You can do the assignment for them. It will get completed without any drama. Everyone will go to

bed at a decent hour and your child will feel happy about turning in their assignment on time without having to struggle through any of the work.

2. You can sit down with your child and guide them through the assignment. It will require time and patience. You might not get to bed early, but your child will feel confident about turning in their assignment knowing that they worked hard on it.

A week later your child comes home from school with another difficult assignment; this one more challenging than the week prior. Again, as the parent you have the choice in how to help your child get through the evening. The child whose parent did the work for them last week is now less capable of completing the new assignment and is going to struggle even more. The child whose parent guided them through the assignment might still need guidance this week, but they will be more capable and confident in getting the work done because they worked hard the week before and successfully completed the assignment.

The parent who chooses to do the assignment for their child is a reflection of Western Medicine. It is quick and easy, but the body becomes dependent on the medication to get better. The parent who chooses to do the hard work and guide their child through a difficult assignment is a reflection of alternative healing. It requires patience and work, but the body learns to heal itself with natural aides, and it grows stronger each time.

Having a balance between Western Medicine and Alternative Healing Methods is important to maintain a healthy lifestyle.

There are times when Western Medicine is crucial to surviving, but we shouldn't become dependent on it for all types of healing. We need to understand the difference between healing and masking the pain.

Below is a list of alternative healing approaches I have benefited from:

- Acupuncture
- Tai Chi
- Energy Clearing with a holistic chiropractor using the NAET Technique
- Energy Clearing with a holistic practitioner using Fork Tuning or Chi Gong
- Young Living Raindrop Massage
- Massage
- Reflexology
- Young Living Essential Oils

Disclaimer: As with all things, there are good and bad practitioners of all kinds. Please be cautious when selecting a practitioner. When possible use recommendations.

A critical element to healing is to remember to take care of yourself. Some people feel the need to be the one to take care of others during a crisis and, in doing so, they often neglect themselves. If this resonates with you, try to keep in mind that you are of most help to others when you are healthy and well balanced.

Another vital aspect to healing is to love yourself. One simple way to love yourself is by taking the time to find something that holds meaning to you and brings you comfort. It should be something that you can easily carry around wherever you go. It can be something as simple as having a memento on you, such as a piece of jewelry or an item that had once belonged to your loved one. It could also be the act of looking at pictures, reading motivational passages, journaling, drawing, photography. Whatever it is, it should be something that is just yours, something you can keep in your possession for times of need.

After my dad died, I did two things which seemed to bring me a sense of peace. I filled a small travel size photo album with pictures of my nieces and nephew, and I carried it with me everywhere I went. When I'd start to feel overwhelmed, I would pull it out and see their bright eyes and big smiles. Looking at these pictures would make me smile, and it would remind me that I was still surrounded by a love that was innocent and pure. My second source of comfort came from wearing a locket which held a picture of my dad and me. In moments when I felt like I needed to hold onto something that was a part of him, I would simply reach for my locket and know that he was there.

Finding solace in another person is natural, but you want to avoid this as your primary source of comfort. We're all human, and we all have our own needs. It is not healthy for one person to carry the burden of being responsible for another person's happiness. It is good to have friends and loved ones who can help you through hard times, but healing is a personal experience that requires a great deal of effort, patience, accountability, and self-awareness. At times the healing process can feel isolating. But find comfort in knowing that by allowing yourself the time and space to truly heal in a healthy way, you will be stronger and more capable of developing healthy relationships with others.

You cannot heal the world until you heal yourself

—Katrina Mayer

Understanding Grief

Signs & Symptoms of Grief

(adapted from Lutheran Hospital—LaCrosse 2001)

It is important to be aware of the signs and symptoms of grief and to know when seeking professional help is needed.

Although the following list may be signs of grief, report those with an asterisk (*) to your physician and or professional counselor.

Physical Effects:

exhaustion/fatigue
aching arms
increased appetite
weight loss or gain
restlessness
dry mouth
*loss of appetite
*sleep problems
*lack of strength/muscle weakness
*breathlessness or shortness of breath
*blurred vision
*palpitations
*headaches

Emotional and/or Psychological Effects:

denial

guilt

anger

resentment

bitterness

irritability

sadness

sense of failure

failure to accept reality

preoccupation with the deceased

fluctuating mood swings

decreased self-esteem

terrible dreams

*persistent depression

*concentration problems

*time confusion

Social Effects:

Prolonged withdrawal from normal activity

Isolation (emotional & physical) from spouse, family,
    and/or friends

In addition to the effects listed above, I would like to add that
it is normal for people who have experienced a traumatic
loss to also exhibit the following behaviors. Some people may
become controlling as a way to deal with what happened,
while others may become reckless. In some situations a person
might even exhibit both.

The Grief Wheel

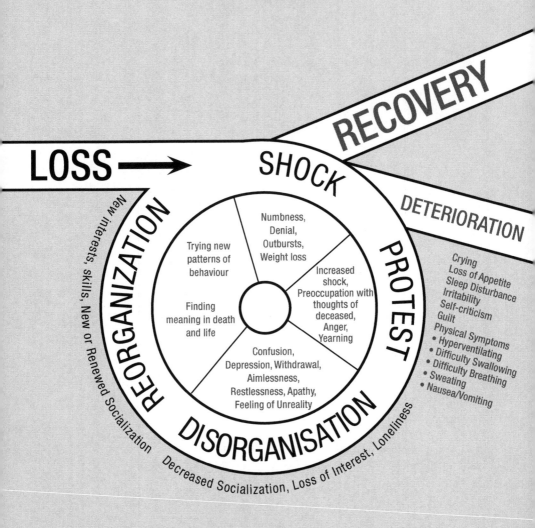

Understanding Grief

I was first introduced to the grief wheel while going through a specialized eight week support group. In theory it made sense.

There are stages that one goes through after experiencing loss, but the reality of grief isn't near as clear and straightforward as this cycle might indicate.

The grieving process can feel frustrating by those who view the grief wheel as an expectation for what should be experienced.

The grieving process does not have clear and defined moments when one might transition from one stage to the next.

As time passes, the grief might become more bearable and bouts of sadness might occur less frequently, but there will always be moments of feeling some sort of loss.

The Grief Landmine

Loss

Denial

Isolation

Guilt

Sadness

Shock

Irritability

Depression

Fear

Protest

Hope

Emotional
Outbursts

Bargaining

Joy

Anger

Disorganization

Panic

Helping
Others

Hope

Guilt

Anger

Recognition

Panic

New
Strengths

Happiness

Sadness

New
Relationships

Recovery

Understanding Grief

Immediately following my dad's death, I often felt like I was about to explode, feeling many different emotions all at once. During my years of attending support groups, I learned this was common amongst most survivors of suicide. This realization lead me to create the Grief Landmine, which I believe is a more accurate depiction of the grieving process.

Loss:	The experience of losing a loved one.
Shock:	Initial disbelief of the loss.
Protest:	Not wanting to believe it is real.
Bargaining:	Thinking of alternative possible outcomes if other actions had been taken.
Disorganization:	Difficulty in interacting with others or functioning in a typical manner.
Recognition:	Beginning to come to terms with the loss.
Recovery:	Moving forward in a healthy manner.

We all know that grief is overwhelming and exhausting; it can be so painful it hurts to breathe. As you move forward in your healing, the grief will become less frequent and more manageable. You will reach a point when life begins to feel "normal" again, and it is during this time that sudden bouts of grief will catch you off guard. As I continued to heal, I was surprised by the guilt I felt during moments when I'd become aware of the fact that I hadn't felt that overwhelming pang of sadness in a while.

It is true that each person will experience their own grief in their own way. The intensity in which one feels grief will vary over the course of healing. We each have our own grief landmine to navigate. But remember that you are not alone and that there is not a right or wrong emotion after experiencing such a loss.

As a culture we are not taught how to appropriately respond to or how to deal with grief. This is even more profound when suicide is involved. Most people don't know what to say, how to say it, or when to say it. Unfortunately because of this, losing a loved one to suicide can often result in also losing people you once considered to be your friends. I don't believe this is an intentional act to further hurt us. I think this phenomenon is due to a lack of understanding on how to best move forward, how to honor the person who passed away, and how to properly communicate with those who have intimately survived the loss.

It is difficult to pinpoint if this is caused by the person who is experiencing the loss, by their friends who don't know how to help them, or a combination of the two. In any case, the result can feel very isolating which can make the grieving process much harder. One way to avoid feeling alone in this process is to attend a support group where you can connect with others who are going through similar struggles.

During my time attending various support groups and discussing the grieving process with survivors of suicide, I noted there are specific experiences which seem to be common among most survivors in regard to the grieving process. For example, most survivors describe the initial pain as feeling unbearable. Along with the intense pain, comes the anticipation that your loved one will walk through the door at any minute. Some people have described the experience of seeing their loved one in dreams or even when they're out in public places.

Another common aspect of grief is that in many ways the second year is the most painful. During the first year the pain is often raw, but because of the shock, there is an odd sense that your loss might not be real. While the all-consuming pain might ease during the first year, it is during the second year that the reality of your loss begins to set in, resulting in a pain many people find to be extremely difficult.

It is often during the second year that survivors are more in tune with each birthday, holiday, or other significant days in which their loved one's presence is painfully missing. Survivors of suicide often talk about the anguish and dread felt in the days or weeks leading up to a day of significance as being more painful than the actual day itself. Whether it is a birthday, holiday, or the anniversary of their loved one's death, survivors are often consumed with the anticipation of the impending pain that will be felt when the actual day arrives. While different aspects of grief might be experienced on that day, it is common for survivors to also experience a sense of relief as they discover the pain is not nearly as bad as they had anticipated.

It is important to consciously note that the grieving process can be devastating. Please take care of yourself. If you find that you are not eating or sleeping regularly, or if you are having trouble functioning at a basic level, please take the necessary steps to get help. Speak to a loved one, a counselor, or your physician. If you don't already know a holistic healer, look for recommendations or research those in your immediate area.

As you go through this grieving process, it is important to remember to drink plenty of water to avoid dehydration which can result from excessive crying.

There are 24-hour crisis lines available to offer support and resources. Check with your local counties for the phone number of the crisis line in your area. If you are in need of support and do not have access to your local crisis line, please call the National Suicide Prevention Lifeline.

National Suicide Prevention Lifeline (24/7):
1-800-273-TALK (8255)

If in an immediate crisis situation, please call **911**.

There is no true healing unless there is a change in outlook, peace of mind and inner happiness.

—Edward Bach

My Story

I was less than two years away from getting my degree in Psychology when my dad died. It is hard to believe that while I was in San Francisco studying the human mind, my dad was roughly 1,800 miles away suffering extreme pain and losing his. Due to the distance between us, I hadn't been aware of how sick he truly was. After his death, I returned to school feeling consumed by the need to understand what happened to him. I made it my goal to learn something new about depression and suicide in every class I took.

As I was nearing graduation, I was asked by a close professor to write a paper about my loss and to present it to the class with the hope that other students could learn from my experience. It was not a mandatory assignment, but she felt that it could be beneficial for me as well as for others. I will admit that I was reluctant to put my thoughts down on paper and even more uncertain about reading those thoughts to an entire class. However, once I did, I was grateful for the experience.

The exercise of writing my story became more than just dictating a series of events. It was a way for me to process what really happened. It was an amazing experience which allowed me the opportunity to make realizations I had not previously been conscious of regarding my dad's situation.

I found that as I was writing and then reading the facts that I had known to be true, I would remember little details that I had somehow stored in my subconscious. Not only did this experience open me up to unconscious thoughts, it freed me from holding it all in.

I will now share my story with you.

My Story
(written and revised many times during the Fall of 2001)

On June 2, 1999, I was a few months shy of turning 21, about two months away from getting married, and on a vacation with my fiancé thinking life couldn't get any better than this. We were in Cancun, Mexico, on a trip given to us as an early wedding gift from my parents. At this same time, my 17-year-old brother, Eric, was also in Cancun with his senior class celebrating their graduation from high school. Our plan was to meet later that day to hang out and see some sights together.

It was still relatively early in the morning and Chris and I were getting ready for the day when our hotel phone rang. Chris answered it and soon after I could tell that there was something wrong. My first thought was that Eric had gotten himself into some kind of trouble. Chris hung up the phone and while walking towards me, he told me that it was my sister's boyfriend calling and that something terrible had happened back home. He took my hands in his and I could tell he was struggling to find the words he needed when he said, "Your dad tried to hang himself."

I began to tremble as his words started to sink in. I asked, "Is he going to be ok? Is he in the hospital?"

Chris pulled me closer to him and, while holding me in his arms, he said, "He didn't make it. He died earlier this morning." I started to pull away from him. I couldn't believe what he was saying.

Chris tried to pull me back into his arms but I pounded on his chest and pushed him away from me. I fell to the bed and began crying and then yelling at him, "But you said that everything would be ok, that he was going to get better. You told me that it would all be ok and it's not! It's not ok!"

My Story

Chris sat beside me, stroking my hair and trying to calm me down. I slowly began to yell less and cry more when I suddenly thought of Eric. Did he know? Was someone in Texas also going to call him? I pulled away from Chris, wiped the tears from my face and said, "We have to get to Eric. I don't want him to hear about this over the phone. I don't want him to be alone when he finds out."

Chris then explained to me that my sister's boyfriend had asked him to find Eric and let him know what had happened. We took a taxi to Eric's hotel. I was a wreck, yelling and pleading with the hotel staff for not allowing Chris and me to enter the hotel due to the fact that we were not official hotel guests. When they finally understood the situation and allowed us to enter, we found that Eric wasn't in his room and none of his friends knew where he was.

Soon after asking his best friend to go look for him, I saw Eric walking up the pathway to his room. I began to cry even more. He looked so happy. It was the first time I had seen him smiling in such a long time. (I would later learn that he had walked down to the beach alone to watch the sun rise). I looked at his smile and the light in his eyes and suddenly I couldn't do it . . . I couldn't tell him. I wanted to be his strong, big sister, but I wasn't strong enough to be the one to take that smile away from him. With great anguish I asked Chris to tell him.

It is a regret that I will carry with me forever, because after Chris stepped out of the room to meet Eric and tell him the news, I realized I needed to be there. By the time I got outside I was too late, Chris had already told him. I wasn't there for him in a way I should have been. I saw his face, the tears swelling in his eyes with a mixture of what looked like fear, pain, and disbelief. I didn't know what to say so I just hugged him.

We didn't say much as we collected our stuff and headed to the airport. Throughout the journey back to my parent's house, I kept thinking that none of this could be real, there had to be a mistake. I also started thinking about my last few days before arriving in Cancun. I had been in Texas for Eric's graduation and for my bridal shower. I had only been there for a long weekend and it had been packed with activities so I didn't get much time with my dad. I didn't think much of it because I knew I was returning to spend time with him after my trip to Cancun.

The last conversation I had with my dad was late at night after he had returned home from work. I remember hugging him and thinking how different his hugs felt. I remember talking to him and thinking how vacant his eyes looked and how flat his words sounded. I remember him telling me, "Jenny, I'm so sorry. I've let everyone down. I've become such a burden on this family since I've gotten sick."

The last time I saw my dad was outside with Chris while Chris was loading our bags into the rental car. I thought it was odd to see him with Chris; because ever since my dad had become sick, he didn't go out of his way to talk to people. Later while driving to the airport, I asked Chris what he and my dad were talking about. He said, "Oh yeah, your dad came out while I was loading the car and said, 'I just want to thank you for loving Jenny as much as you do. I'm happy knowing that she will be with you, and I know that you will take good care of her.' That was pretty much all he said and then he went back in the house."

As soon as Chris finished telling me what my dad said to him, I knew there was something wrong. I was a daddy's girl to a dad who was not overly thrilled with the idea of his baby girl getting married so young. I immediately called home. My mom answered and told me my dad was sleeping. I begged her to put him on the phone. I knew he wasn't really sleeping—one of the side effects of the anti-depressants he was on was that he couldn't sleep. I begged and pleaded for him to come to the phone but when she wouldn't get him I said, "Please tell him I love him. Promise me you'll tell him that I love him and I'll be back in a few days." I hung up knowing there was something wrong but I never imagined he would die.

The trip home from Cancun was a long one; full of tears and unbearable silence. What do you say after hearing such news? Where do you begin and how do you make enough sense of it to talk about it? When we finally arrived at my parent's house, I rushed into what was normally a loud and chaotic atmosphere. But not that day; on that day the house was hushed, it had never been so quiet. As I came in, I saw my mom sitting on the couch surrounded by people I didn't know. I just stood there looking around this space that I had grown up in and yet it felt so foreign to me now.

It was then that I saw a gentleman approaching me. I recognized him from my parent's church. He came over as if he was going to hug me. Then he put his hand on my shoulder and said, "You don't have to worry. Your dad isn't going to hell." I didn't know if I was going to punch him or throw up. I was overwhelmed with so much anger at that moment that I couldn't even see straight.

Fortunately for both of us, my older brother walked over and pulled me away. He hugged me while I cried. He held me in his arms and hugged me the tightest he had ever held me before. I don't know how much time passed before I realized that my other two brothers were also there; all of us holding each other up, all of us trying not to fall.

As I remained in my parent's house over the next few days, I found myself always looking up when the front door would open, thinking that my dad would come walking through, but obviously it never happened. I kept asking myself how this could have happened. He was my dad. He was the person I went to when I needed something. MY dad couldn't do something like this.

My heart still aches over my dad's death, and for the pain that he must have been feeling before he died. I can't even begin to imagine the amount of torment he must have been enduring to push him to take his own life. Even though I knew he was sick, and for months we all watched him deteriorate, I never imagined that my dad would commit suicide.

While my dad's death was tragic, good things have come from it. His death has inspired me to learn more about depression and how serious it can be. I have become very passionate about suicide awareness and prevention. Through the classes I have taken and the research I've done, I know that what happened to my dad wasn't his fault. He was sick and his illness killed him.

My studies have helped me to look at my dad's depression the same way one might look at cancer. His depression slowly but surely ate away at him until there was nothing left–it took over his body and mind. My dad fought the battle as long as he could, but he knew, as we all did, that he was no longer the man we grew up with. He had lost the ability to love life and the plea-sures that came with it. He had lost the ability to make rational decisions.

I have now participated in both individual and group therapy in an attempt to fully work through all that has happened in the last two years. Through therapy and my studies, I have become certain of one thing. That is I cannot change that he died nor can I continue to wish that I could have done something that would have saved him. I miss him every day and I wish I still had him to talk to and laugh with. But I know that even if he were still alive, I would still miss him. I have missed my dad far longer than when he died on June 2, 1999. It was while writing this, "My Story," I realized that the depression my dad suffered from had taken over who he was, and had killed the dad I knew long before his physical death took place.

Exercise 1: Write Your Story

For some, the act of writing your story may feel like a pointless activity because you already know your own story. For others, this exercise might seem daunting; it might feel too painful to put your experience on paper. Putting it on paper makes it too real. While writing the events of your loss might elicit different emotions for different people, it is intended to provide you the opportunity to ultimately feel relief by the emotional release which takes place during such a process.

Writing your story is an emotional process, and one that needs to be given the appropriate setting and time. I would encourage you to find a quiet space where you can be free in your thoughts, take a pen and paper or sit at your computer and just write. Write like no one will ever read it. Don't worry about spelling or mistakes. Treat this experience as an ongoing process rather than a one-time assignment. This is something you will want to read and edit over a period of days, maybe even weeks or months.

When you stand and share your story in an empowering way, your story will heal you and your story will heal somebody else.

—Iyanla Vanzant

Understanding Emotions

While navigating your own grieving process, please try to keep in mind that emotional responses are not the same for everyone. While two people may have experienced the same loss, they might be experiencing it in different ways. During the healing process, it is imperative that you focus on your own emotions and not compare yourself with anyone else or judge others for what they are feeling. There is not a right or wrong, normal or abnormal reaction to loss as long as it is not harmful to you or to others.

Psychologist, W. Gerrod Parrot believed that there were six Primary Emotions and that each of those have Secondary and Tertiary Emotions. On the next two pages is a modified version of Parrot's list of emotions.

Understanding our emotions can help us to better navigate our responses when interacting with others. It is also beneficial to realize that we have the ability to feel multiple emotions at the same time. I have found it helpful to embrace each emotion for what it is and to allow myself the time and space to fully experience it, try to understand it, and move forward in a healthy way.

1. Fear

Alarm	Horror	Terror
Anxiety	Hysteria	Uneasiness
Apprehension	Mortification	Worry
Distress	Nervousness	Terror
Dread	Panic	
Fright	Shock	

2. Sadness

Agony	Grief	Pity
Alienation	Guilt	Regret
Anguish	Homesickness	Rejection
Defeatism	Humiliation	Remorse
Dejection	Hurt	Shame
Depression	Insecurity	Sorrow
Despair	Insult	Suffering
Disappointment	Isolation	Sympathy
Dismay	Loneliness	Unhappy
Displeasure	Melancholy	Woe
Embarrassment	Misery	
Gloom	Neglect	

3. Anger

Aggravation	Frustration	Rage
Agitation	Fury	Resentment
Annoyance	Grouchy	Revulsion
Bitter	Grumpy	Scorn
Contempt	Hatred	Spite
Crosspatch	Hostility	Torment
Disgust	Irritability	Torment
Dislike	Jealousy	Vengefulness
Envy	Loathing	Wrath
Exasperation	Outrage	

4. Surprise

Amazement
Astonishment

5. Joy

Amusement	Euphoria	Optimism
Bliss	Excitement	Pleasure
Cheerfulness	Exhilaration	Pride
Contentment	Gaiety	Rapture
Delight	Gladness	Relief
Eagerness	Glee	Satisfaction
Ecstasy	Happiness	Thrill
Elation	Hope	Triumph
Enjoyment	Jolliness	Zeal
Enthrallment	Joviality	Zest
Enthusiasm	Jubilation	

6. Love

Adoration	Desire
Affection	Fondness
Attractiveness	Infatuation
Caring	Liking
Compassion	Longing

One Death, Six Responses

I am one of six children. With permission from my siblings, I will share each of our immediate responses to our dad's death in order to demonstrate the effect of how the loss of one person can impact six different people. Even though some of us felt the same emotion, we felt it for different reasons. Each of us had a different relationship with our dad, and each of us had been personally affected by his depression in different ways.

Emotions felt in 1999—
Immediately following our dad's death

Tammy
(26 years)

No shared response

Sarah
(24 years)
I was in shock that he killed himself and I was sad that he was gone. But it was the feelings of guilt from wanting it to be over that were the most painful. It had gotten so hard to be around him and to deal with his depression. On different occasions leading up to his death, I had found myself wishing he would just die. I never thought he would actually commit suicide, but I wanted all the pain to stop for him and for those of us who were around him.

Jeff
(22 years)
I would have to say that I was primarily feeling confusion and disbelief. I just kept asking myself, 'How did it come to this—how could he do this?' The pain was unbearable.

Jenny
(20 years)

I felt intense disbelief and sadness. But more than anything, I felt guilty for not realizing how sick he truly was.

Eric
(17 years)

I felt guilty in my own way. I was around all the time and yet I wasn't really around. It was my senior year and I guess I kept myself pretty busy as a way to avoid being home. I knew he was sick, it was hard to be around him, but I never thought suicide was a possibility. When he died all I could think was that I could have done more, I could have been around more to help. Shortly before my graduation trip to Cancun, I found out that there was need for one more chaperone. Now normally I wouldn't be the one to ask my parents to chaperone, especially on a trip to Cancun. But it's like I knew he was getting worse, so I went to him and I asked him to go. I told him that he needed to get away for a little bit and just go somewhere where he could relax and start to feel good again. He told me that he didn't think he could handle going on the trip. I didn't push him—I just walked away accepting his answer. After he died, I couldn't help but wonder if he would still be alive if I had just not taken 'no' for an answer. I should have pushed a little harder. I should have done more to help him get better.

Lance
(15 years)

In the beginning, I was sad and then I was pissed off and disappointed. He thought he was doing us a favor; but really he just put us in a worse situation. When he died, I felt oblivious from what everyone else was going through. I just kept doing what I was doing and no one in the family really talked about what happened. In a way, I understand why no one was talking to me because I wasn't talking to them either. I found it easier to talk to my friends about it because they weren't as involved or affected by what happened. They had the ability to be objective and the ability to just listen. I was so young . . . we should have talked more.

Emotions felt in 2014—
15 years after our dad's death

Tammy
(41 years)
No shared response

Sarah
(39 years)

I'm sad and hurting. I sometimes find myself wondering what life would be like if he was still alive. I truly believe so much of this life would be better if he was still here to handle different situations. I miss him every day–some days are harder than others. I want so badly to speak to him, to hear his voice, and to hear his thoughts. But more than anything, I want to feel his arms around me while he tells me everything will be ok.

Jeff
(37 years)

I'm at peace with his death and with knowing that he is no longer in pain. After going through my own hell with antidepressants, knowing how crazy and out of control they made me feel, I have a much better understanding of what dad was going through, and I can understand how he did what he did. He was no longer in control. Looking back on the time leading up to his death also brings me peace. I truly believe I said and did everything

I could to help him, but I realize it wasn't enough and that's not my fault. I feel fortunate that he and I had time together before he died. We were able to repair what was once a very broken relationship. At the time of his death, I could honestly call him my friend.

Jenny
(35 years)

I'm currently at the greatest state of peace since losing my dad. Through my own trials and struggles, I have recently reconnected with my dad in a way that not only honors his memory but also allows me to feel close to him again. His death has had an incredible impact on who I am today, and while it hasn't always been easy, I'm grateful for all that I have learned and the person I've become.

Eric
(32 years)

I don't really know how I feel now. I guess you could say that, after everything I've gone through with my own depression over the last few years, I understand how he was able to do what he did."

Lance
(30 years)

I don't think of it much, but when I do it still pisses me off that he chose that route. People are always telling me that he would be proud of me. If he wanted to be proud of me, he should have stuck around. I recently went through my own depression so I understand and see why he did what he did. But I wish he could have been stronger. I'm not sure I've really had the opportunity to process what happened. In a way, I was forced to accept it quickly because I had to help take care of Mom and Jeff. Acceptance is key—death is a part of life. I don't dwell on it.

Speaking to each of my siblings for this piece was difficult, and yet I feel truly blessed for having done it.

I found that asking each of my brothers to participate was an awkward and somewhat challenging conversation to start, but I was pleasantly surprised by how open each of them was. There wasn't even a hint of hesitation from them in answering my questions. It was during this time that I realized how little I have spoken to them about my dad's death. It also revealed how disconnected we've been in understanding how each one of us has been impacted.

The conversations I had with my brothers helped me to see their individual pain and hardships. Until now, I had really only known my own. I had assumptions of what they must have gone through and how it must have for them. However, after hearing them describe their own experience from that day I realized that my perception and their reality were very different.

My conversations with my sisters were much more strained and challenging. This came as a surprise to me because I had initially felt more comfortable starting the conversation with them. They both agreed to participate but asked for time to reflect before getting back to me.

Sarah struggled with sharing her emotions for this piece. I believe her reluctance to share was largely due to the fact that she felt guilty for how she felt, and she didn't want to feel judged for feeling it. She became overwhelmed with emotion each time I brought it up. Eventually I asked her if I could write about what I remembered us discussing the day of our dad's funeral for her initial response, and the things she had written about him on Facebook in the last few years for her current response. After reading what I had written on her behalf, she hesitantly agreed to allow me to use it.

I attempted to assure Sarah that what she had felt was a common response. By openly sharing about the guilt she felt for wanting it to be over, she would be helping others know that they are not alone, and they don't have to feel ashamed or hold on to their feelings of guilt. I want her and everyone else who feels this pain to know that we can't control how we feel. It is natural to want difficult times in our lives to come to an end.

I have been to several support group meetings where there has been someone in attendance who was not only struggling with the loss of their loved one to suicide, but also with the fact that their immediate reaction was relief. For people like me, who were not immediately impacted by our loved one's depression, the suicide comes as a complete shock. For someone like Sarah, who saw our dad wither away on a daily basis and was impacted regularly by his depression, the suicide, while still a shock, can provide an odd sense of closure to what has been a stressful and uncertain time. This feeling of closure does not prevent them from feeling the pain . . . for many, it seems to magnify it.

While I believe Tammy wanted to support me in this endeavor, she was not in a place where she felt she could openly share. I anxiously waited for two years hoping she would offer me her thoughts and that her contribution would resonate with a reader. During a discussion with a friend, I realized Tammy's inability to participate was, in fact, her contribution, and it would most certainly resonate with a reader.

My desire to have a written response from each of my siblings had inhibited me from remembering that some people might not be ready to talk about the death of their loved one. We all need to remember to be considerate of the fact that everyone has their own timeline for working through their grief and processing the events that took place.

Exercise 2: Identifying Your Own Emotions

1. If needed, review the list of emotions from the start of this chapter and then write down the emotions that most accurately reflect what you felt at the time of your loved one's death. Take the time to dive deeper by trying to understand why you might have felt the emotions you felt.

2. Have your emotions changed over time? If yes, what do you feel has contributed most to your emotions evolving? Are you currently feeling the emotions you would like to be feeling when you think of your loved one?

she needs time, like we
all do. time to be ok
with being ok.
because sometimes feeling
right after feeling
so wrong for so long,
is the hardest
thing to get used to.

—JmStorm

Three Questions

A common topic of conversation discussed during support group meetings has been about the questions survivors of suicide are asked after losing their loved one. Not everyone you interact with is going to be comfortable asking about your loss. But for those who are, there seems to be three questions that almost always come up.

1.   How did your loved one die?
2.   Did you know or suspect that your loved one was struggling with depression?
3.   Did your loved one leave a note?

During the various meetings I've attended, I've become aware that many people tend to have a set answer ready for when these questions are asked. I am the type of person who feels comfortable sharing personal information. However, I've relied on a set response during times when I've felt vulnerable and wanted to maintain control of my emotions.

It is good to remember that just because someone is comfortable asking these or any other questions, it doesn't mean that you should feel obligated to provide a response beyond what you feel comfortable sharing. It is more than alright to tell someone that you do not wish to talk about the details.

My Answers

Question 1: How did he die?

My dad died by hanging himself in the carport of the home where I grew up.

Question 2: Did you know or suspect that he was struggling with depression?

Yes, but I never thought he would die by suicide.

My dad was a chemist at a utility company where he was required to do an annual breathing test. In 1997 he failed his breathing test ultimately resulting in a diagnosis of Sarcoidosis, which is an autoimmune condition that can result in organ failure. The treatment protocol involved a heavy dose of steroids and within a few months he started showing signs of depression. It was roughly two years from the time he was diagnosed with Sarcoidosis to the time of his death.

In November 1998, about seven months before my dad died, he went to his employer and asked to be hospitalized. My dad informed his boss he was concerned that without proper medical treatment he would die. Unfortunately, it was decided that it would cost the company too much money to seek such treatment. Instead of being hospitalized, he was given one month leave to recover with the help of a psychiatrist. The psychiatrist working with my dad prescribed six different antidepressants in the six months leading up to his death.

After my dad died and the reality started to set in that his open request for help had been dismissed, I often found myself asking, "How many mornings had he woken up, gone through his normal routine of getting ready, walked out the back door, and looked upon the spot where he would ultimately die? How many times had he walked out that door thinking he **would** die but then manage to make it through one more day?"

On June 2, 1999, he was no longer strong enough to fight the illness that consumed him. He got dressed in his regular work clothes, walked out the back door, and hung himself in the carport. It was my older brother, Jeff, who came home early that morning and found him hanging. It is Jeff who will forever have to carry the burden of that image. The rest of us can speculate but none of us will ever fully be aware of what he had to see or what he had to go through when he found our dad.

Question 3: Did he leave a note?

Yes, we discovered that he had actually written multiple notes, including a letter which had been written a couple of weeks before he died. The letter addressed each member of our family with a personal message. A final note was found in the master bathroom the morning of his death.

Healing comes in waves
and maybe today
the waves hit the rocks
and that ok, that's ok, darling,
you are still healing
you are still healing.

—Ijeoma Umebinyuo

His letters

December 1998 (typed with handwritten signature)
I believe the Prozac was keeping me from sleeping and the lack of sleep was making me into a walking zombie. I couldn't possibly go on like that. On the other hand, it must have been doing some good at relieving the depression, because I am certainly becoming more depressed with each passing day. Now that I am on the new medicine, I am not as detached, but I have been having heart palpitations—and I am definitely still "not with the program." I still feel detached, but now in a different way. My vision is still blurry and I feel terrible. I have been fighting this for over two weeks now, and I don't feel like I am any better. I would have to say that I am worse than I was yesterday and the day before, but not as bad as I was Monday or the few days before that. What I am missing is hope. I have given up believing that the medicine will make me better, and I know that the problems that put me into this condition are not going away just because I wish they would.

I'm sorry. My job is in jeopardy even without this other stuff, and I can't continue like this. I hope you can forgive me.

I love you. There are no words to describe how wonderful I think you are.

I love our children and grandchildren. Next to you they are my best friends.

I pray that God will give all of you strength and wisdom. Love, Scott

Thursday, February 4, 1999 (typed)
I got better because I had hope that things were getting better. I can't go through this again.

Sunday, February 7, 1999 (typed)
All of this is subject to change with the court proceeding. I'm sorry. I hope you can forgive me.

I love you. There are no words to describe how wonderful I think you are.

I love our children and grandchildren. Next to you they are my best friends.

I pray that God will give all of you strength and wisdom.

March 28, 1999 (typed)
My dad wrote a five page letter to my mom explaining all the legal information she would need to be aware of upon the time of his death, including details about life insurance, social security, health benefits, house and car payments, etc.

April 11, 1999 (typed)
I started this note on the 6th of December. I have just reread it and am amazed at how much things are still the same.

Any objective evaluation of my condition would say that I am getting worse. I have watched you trying to help and have felt so guilty because I can't respond. There is only so much that anyone can take and I know that I am reaching my limit. I know that you must be reaching yours, too. If you are reading this note, times are going to be hard for you for a while, and I am truly sorry.

April 26, 1999 (handwritten)
I can't work and I can't think. And I'm not sure if the pain is physical or mental.

I wish only the best for each of you, and I feel like I am keeping you from being able to move ahead with your lives.

I have been desperate and confused for months. Please forgive me for not being able to do better.

Date written unknown but believed to have been written in April or May of 1999 (handwritten)
My will and life insurance are in the third drawer of the old filing cabinet.

The medicines have helped and hurt. When I am not depressed I cannot sleep. I am sorry. It's just too much. And I know how hard it is on the rest of you.

I love all of you. I have been depressed for 5 months and I know it has been hard on all of you. I am afraid I am losing my grip on reality. I have said I'm living in the Twilight Zone and I know it's getting worse.

Please forgive me for not being able to deal with this.

May 25, 1999 (typed)
I have never been very good at putting my feelings into words. To do so now means I run the risk of saying the wrong thing or leaving something important unsaid.

Terri, you have been my best friend and the inspiration for my accomplishments. Whatever good things I have done, you have been my motivation. I have taken the greatest pleasure in sharing peaceful moments with you. I know you feel inadequate in some things, but your strengths have always far outweighed your weaknesses—and I know that you are loved for your tender heart and helping spirit. There are just no words to express the depth of my love, admiration, respect and concern for you.

Tammy, you have bettered me at my own game. You are intelligent and capable and driven. I marvel at your success. Like many oldest siblings, you have combined many of the best qualities of your mother and me and made something better. I know you will teach them to Marissa.

Sarah, you have the kind and sensitive nature that endears us all to you. I know that in time you will be able to use your intelligence, academic gifts, and healing instincts. Cherish Cole and Makayla while they are young. I made the mistake of waiting until you grew up to learn how to relate to you.

Jeff, you have become a dear friend in these months of adversity. We spent some of the best days of my life together, and I only regret that I didn't appreciate them and you more at the time. You proved to be stronger than I ever imagined possible.

Jenny, you live your life with incredible passion. Thank you for sharing it with the rest of us.

Eric, you have been the quiet one. I often underestimated your talents and the strength of your personality, even at those times I have been so proud of your accomplishments. You have never ceased to brighten my days.

Lance, you have been kindness and support. I know there are times when you must get tired of being helpful and considerate, but I am truly thankful that you are that way.

I know this leaves too much unsaid. I am proud of you, and I love each of you more than words can express.

Unfortunately, the last note containing his final thoughts has been lost. I hold out hope that one day I will find it.

What I remember from his final note was him explaining that he had waited for Tammy and me to return for Eric's graduation so we could all be together one last time, that he was no longer strong enough to keep going and that he was sorry.

There is no greater agony than bearing an untold story inside you.

—Maya Angelou

Healing Properties of Writing a Letter

For those of us who have lost a loved one suddenly, the pain and sadness we feel is often accompanied by the feeling that too much was left unsaid. Writing a letter to the person you lost gives you an opportunity to say all that was left unsaid, and it can assist you with your healing.

For the purpose of this exercise, I will share with you the first letter I wrote to my dad while I was participating in a specialized process group a few months after he died.

My Letter
(written May 17, 2000)

Dear Dad,

Today I'm going to my support group and I'm supposed to bring a letter I've written to you. When I was given the assignment, I had no idea it would be so hard to do. I have put it off as long as possible and now I find myself sitting at school trying to write you a letter, and all I can think about is the fact that tomorrow would have been your birthday. You would be turning 49 and I would be giving you a hard time about getting old.

We would have laughed and I would be wishing that I could be home to celebrate with you. But you're gone and I'm alone. You were my family. You were the one who loved me. You were the one who wanted a better life for me. You were the one who pushed me out of my comfort zone. You were the one who made me recognize my faults and deal with them. You weren't always nice but you were always honest. You had high expectations and I feel like I disappointed you.

*I forgot your birthday last year and I feel horrible. Some-
times I wonder if I added to your depression by the choices
I was making. I still remember when I was 17, calling home
from school, and I was surprised when it was you who
answered. I was a senior and it was my free period. I called
home to ask Mom a question but for the life of me I don't
remember what it was. What I do remember was having
a strange conversation with you. You sounded exasperat-
ed when you said, "Jenny, promise me something. Promise
me that you'll go to college and make something of yourself.
Promise me that you won't get married until you're at least 25,
and promise me that you'll get married for the right reasons."*

*I promised you that I would do all that you were asking.
I thought you were being odd but I also thought it shouldn't
be too hard to do. But then I broke one of those promises.
I was in college, I was happy and working hard; but by the
age of 20, I had agreed to get married. I was so excited until
I returned home and had dinner with you. You looked at
me and with no emotion in your face or voice you said, "I'd
rather go to a baseball game than your wedding and you
know how I feel about baseball."*

*I was crushed but I can't say I was surprised by your
response. I was caught up in the excitement of being in love
and I tried to convince you that, while I knew I was breaking
the promise of not waiting until I was 25, I was still honor-
ing all of the other promises I made. It didn't matter . . . we
were different after that day, and then you died weeks before
my wedding. I guess you really didn't want to go.*

*I sometimes wonder if you would still be alive if I hadn't
gotten married. I wonder if you knew how much I loved you.
I wonder if you are looking down on me now and, if so, do I
make you proud?*

*Sometimes I just want to scream. I want to hit something
or someone. I want you to still be here! I want to celebrate your*

birthday with you. I want you to know I got all As the semester before you died and all As since then. I want you to know that I miss you and I wish you were still a phone call away.

I need to know what happened. I need to know that something good will come from losing you. I need to know that I won't always feel this way. I need to know that you are ok.

I love you and I will do everything I can to turn your death into something good. Thank you for pushing me, for challenging me, for supporting me. Thank you for loving me. Thank you for being my dad.

Love, Jenny

Exercise 3: Write Your Letter

Use the process of writing letters as an opportunity to say the things you didn't have the chance to say, to ask the questions you don't have answers to, and to express whatever feelings might be consuming you. The intention of this process is not to give the letters to anyone; it is meant to be used as a therapeutic tool to help you release the negative energy you're holding on to.

It is not uncommon for your personal relationships to be strained while dealing with the loss of a loved one to suicide. Using this method of writing letters without delivering them can be beneficial in those situations as well. I have written several letters to my dad, but the letters that have allowed me the most relief are the letters I have written to my mom. Even before my dad died, my mom and I had a challenging relationship. The intensity of our struggles only worsened after his death. Writing letters to my mom but never sending them to her has given me an outlet to say what I need to say without hurting her or causing more stress on an already strained relationship.

Life is like riding a bicycle. To keep your
balance, you must keep moving.

—Albert Einstein

Overcoming the Stigma

For those of us who have lost a loved one to suicide, we go through a much different process of grieving than someone who has lost a loved one to any other illness, natural causes, or an accident. We have to sort through the reality of what has happened. We often need time to process the suicide before we have the ability to even truly grieve for the person we've lost.

The pain of trying to process losing a loved one to suicide is often compounded by the way society views and responds to depression and suicide. While depression and suicide are being discussed more openly, there remains a stigma associated with this illness and this cause of death. Unlike most other illnesses, depression is often seen by others as a choice or as a weakness. Therefore, there is often a sense of blame and judgment involved when a person dies by suicide.

In 2002, I was hired by a crisis center to be a crisis counselor and a community educator. This position involved answering calls on the suicide hotline as well as going to schools and community events to give presentations on suicide awareness and prevention. During the initial stages of creating my presentation, I realized there was another illness that carried a similar stigma.

If you think back to the 1980s and reflect on the way in which our society treated those who had contracted the AIDS virus, it is similar to the way we currently treat those who are struggling with depression and those who have lost a loved one to suicide. Even if it is unintentional, people often don't know how to respond to admissions of depression or stories of suicide. They distance themselves, and they often think, "That will never happen to me or anyone I care about."

The sad truth is that while the AIDS virus can only impact those who have contracted it, depression can impact anyone at any time. This got me thinking . . . if we were to look at depression more like we view cancer, maybe we would have healthier results in treating those who suffer from it. In addition to that, maybe bystanders would be more understanding and supportive.

Just like with cancer, depression has various stages.

Cancer—Stage 1 involves early detection, working with a doctor, and implementing the necessary treatment. It typically has a positive outcome.

Cancer—Stage 2 is more complicated and it requires more steps to achieve a positive outcome. But it still has good odds for the person to return to a healthy lifestyle.

Cancer—Stage 3 is much harder to address and it often takes a team of doctors and therapies, along with more time, to potentially have a positive outcome.

Cancer—Stage 4 is the scariest and hardest to treat. The doctors are relying on each other as well as new and alternative treatments. Statistically the survival rate with stage 4 cancer is very low.

Depression works the same way. If we are living healthy lives and are able to recognize the early signs of Stage 1 Depression, it is much easier to get the necessary help to return to a happy and healthy life. If we are unable to recognize or admit that we have depression, and we wait until it is stage 3 or 4, then getting help is much more complicated and difficult. No matter what stage we're at when we detect the depression, if we are unable to receive the proper care or we're unwilling to seek help, our depression can evolve into Stage 4, resulting in a low survival rate.

Exercise 4: Recognize the Symptoms

In order to be your own best advocate, it is important that you are able to recognize the difference between sadness and depression. Please take the time to review this list and note if there are any symptoms that are causing you ongoing issues.

Symptoms of Depression
by The Mayo Clinic
http://www.mayoclinic.org/diseases-conditions/depression/basics/symptoms/con-20032977 (as at 4/13/2017)

Although depression may occur only one time during your life, usually people have multiple episodes of depression. During these episodes, symptoms occur most of the day, nearly every day, and may include:
- Feelings of sadness, tearfulness, emptiness or hopelessness
- Angry outbursts, irritability, or frustration, even over small matters
- Loss of interest or pleasure in most or all normal activities, such as sex, hobbies, or sports
- Sleep disturbances, including insomnia or sleeping too much
- Tiredness and lack of energy, so even small tasks take extra effort
- Changes in appetite — often reduced appetite and weight loss, but increased cravings for food and weight gain in some people
- Anxiety, agitation, or restlessness
- Slowed thinking, speaking, or body movements
- Feelings of worthlessness or guilt, fixating on past failures or blaming yourself for things that aren't your responsibility

- Trouble thinking, concentrating, making decisions, and remembering things
- Frequent or recurrent thoughts of death, suicidal thoughts, suicide attempts, or suicide
- Unexplained physical problems, such as back pain or headaches

For many people with depression, symptoms usually are severe enough to cause noticeable problems in day-to-day activities, such as work, school, social activities, or relationships with others. Other people may feel generally miserable or unhappy without really knowing why.

Depression symptoms in children and teens
Common signs and symptoms of depression in children and teenagers are similar to those of adults, but there can be some differences.

- In younger children, symptoms of depression may include sadness, irritability, clinginess, worry, aches and pains, refusing to go to school, or being underweight
- In teens, symptoms may include sadness, irritability, feeling negative and worthless, anger, poor performance or poor attendance at school, feeling misunderstood and extremely sensitive, using drugs or alcohol, eating or sleeping too much, self-harm, loss of interest in normal activities, and avoidance of social interaction

Children with attention-deficit/hyperactivity disorder (ADHD) can demonstrate irritability without sadness or loss of interest. However, major depression can occur with ADHD.

Depression symptoms in older adults

Depression is not a normal part of growing older, and it should never be taken lightly. Unfortunately, depression often goes undiagnosed and untreated in older adults, and they may feel reluctant to seek help. Symptoms of depression may be different or less obvious in older adults, such as:

- Memory difficulties or personality changes
- Physical aches or pain
- Fatigue, loss of appetite, sleep problems, aches or loss of interest in sex — not caused by a medical condition or medication
- Often wanting to stay at home, rather than going out to socialize or doing new things
- Suicidal thinking or feelings, especially in older men

When to see a doctor

If you feel depressed, make an appointment to see your doctor as soon as you can. If you're reluctant to seek treatment, talk to a friend or loved one, a health care professional, a faith leader, or someone else you trust.

When to get emergency help

If you think you may hurt yourself or attempt suicide, call 911 or your local emergency number immediately.

Also consider these options if you're having suicidal thoughts:

- Call your mental health specialist
- Call a suicide hotline number — in the U.S., call the National Suicide Prevention Lifeline at 1-800-273-TALK (1-800-273-8255). Use that same number and press "1" to reach the Veterans Crisis Line

- Seek help from your primary doctor or other health care provider
- Reach out to a close friend or loved one
- Contact a minister, spiritual leader, or someone else in your faith community

If a loved one or friend is in danger of attempting suicide or has made an attempt:

- Make sure someone stays with that person
- Call 911 or your local emergency number immediatelyOr, if you can do so safely, take the person to the nearest hospital emergency room

When "I" is replaced by "we" even illness becomes wellness.

—Author Unknown

The Power of Words

It was after losing my dad that I truly became aware of the power of words . . . especially when it comes to suicide.

After my dad died, it was difficult for me to be around people who would joke or make comments about killing themselves when they were having a bad day. *Shoot me* or *I could just kill myself* have become common phases by people who are often trying to be funny about their frustrations. For those of us who have lost someone to suicide, those phrases hold power and that power often stirs up raw emotions. I have attended college classes and church services where the presenter has made such comments as a way to make light of the subject. While I'm in a healthy place in regards to my own loss, those moments tear at my heart for anyone else who might be in attendance, who may have just lost a loved one, or has never had the support to heal from losing their loved one.

In those moments, I want to shout to the world, "Why do you have to be so insensitive!" I feel compelled to speak up and try to enlighten those around me. It hasn't always been easy. In those instances, I do my best to regain my composure and approach the presenter to let them know that I understood they were trying to be funny, but in their attempt to add a little humor, they actually caused me to feel uncomfortable and truly sad. Sad that I lost my dad, sad that there are potentially others who were hurt by those words, and most of all, sad that we as a society do not provide the proper support and understanding for those who struggle with depression and suicide.

Beyond asking people to be more sensitive and not joke about suicide, there are a few phrases I would like to have removed from our speech when talking about suicide.

The terms *successful suicide* and *failed suicide* are used as a way to describe if a person completed suicide versus attempted suicide. I was a young adult when my dad died, but I will never forget attending a support group and the facilitator used the phrase, *successful suicide*. In my mind, I couldn't understand how anyone could use those two words together. There was nothing successful about suicide.

I brought this up later in a private therapy session and I was told that the more considerate term to use is *completed suicide*. While it only changed one word it was amazing how much it impacted the emotions I felt. Instead of being angry at the idea that someone would consider suicide as being successful, I was able to focus my energy on processing the fact that the suicide happened.

I was fortunate to participate in an incredible process group where we not only talked about who we lost, how they died, and the pain it caused, but we were also taught techniques that could assist us in our healing. One simple way to help move past the anger, resentment, and frustration that comes from losing a loved one to suicide is to change the way we talk about how they died.

A few more common phases that are used when talking about suicide are–*he chose to kill himself, he took his life, he killed himself,* or *he committed suicide.* These phrases do not reflect that our loved ones had an illness or that the illness was responsible for their death. Recognizing their illness and their death as a result of an illness allows us to move forward in grieving the person we lost. One way to honor that recognition is to rephrase the common ways of discussing a suicidal death by saying, "He or she died from suicide." While this might not seem like much, what it does is remove any inclination of blame or judgment toward the person who died.

As you progress through your journey please remember to be considerate of those around you and trust that each person has their own struggle to face. I would encourage each of you to stay true to who you are, speak up for yourself and the person you lost, and most importantly, love yourself and know that the death of the person you lost is not a reflection of who you are or what you did or didn't do for them.

> **Exercise 5: Change the Way You Speak About Depression & Suicide**
>
> Be mindful of the words you are speaking when discussing your loved one. Find the courage and strength to educate others on how the words we use can impact our views and actions. Challenge yourself and those around you to change the way we talk about depression and suicide. In order to successfully remove the stigma associated with suicide, we must recognize that depression is an illness and suicide is a deadly result if not properly treated.
>
> | Phrases to Avoid | Encouraged Phrases |
> |---|---|
> | Successful suicide | Completed suicide |
> | He is choosing to feel that way | He is struggling with depression |
> | He took his own life | I lost him to suicide |
> | She committed suicide | She died from suicide |
> | He killed himself | Depression caused his death |
> | She gave up / She chose the easy route | She lost her battle with depression |

Always make sure to pick your words, for your words can hurt or heal.

—Author Unknown

Suicide—What It Is and What It Isn't

I was recently talking to my daughters about suicide as my thirteen-year-old was preparing for a forum discussion at school on the subject of assisted suicide. I realized I have spent the last few years openly discussing suicide with them in a manner in which I believe to be healthy. However, I haven't shared with them the stigma of suicide and that some people view suicide as being an act of selfishness or cowardice. I asked them if they have heard other people talk about suicide and, if so, what have they heard.

My ten-year-old daughter told me there are different kinds of suicide. She went on to say, "There is the kind of suicide bad people use to hurt or kill other people, then there is suicide that happens to sick people like your dad."

My thirteen-year-old then chimed in by saying, "There is also assisted suicide for people who are really sick and going to die anyway."

We then had a short discussion about the various types of suicide. This encounter reminded me of another conversation I had with survivors of suicide years ago when we also discussed the various types of suicide and how it can add to the stigma that suicide is a choice.

I personally believe there are three types of suicide. There are mission-based suicides, assisted suicides, and depression-induced suicides. Mission-based suicides are when someone has been trained or programmed to carry out orders in the name of their country, their religion, or their cause. This type of suicide almost always involves harming or killing other targets.

In 1997, Oregon was the first state to pass a law in favor of assisted suicide, also known as death with dignity. Since then four other states have implemented laws to protect doctors who offer aide to a patient who has been diagnosed with a terminal illness. Each state has its own set of guidelines that are required for this course of action to be considered legal medical care.

Depression-induced suicide has the stigma that suicide is a choice. This is the result of a misunderstood illness—an illness which is also often perceived as a choice. The public perception of depression-induced suicide is complicated by the fact that not everyone who struggles with depression shows the same signs, nor do they all use the same method to die. This point of view is intensified by the suicides which involve the murder of others.

Depression-induced suicides are the result of a mental illness becoming terminal. The person's ability to make rational decisions has become significantly impaired. From personal experience, I can speak to the fear I felt when I transitioned from depression to feeling suicidal. My depression made me feel helpless and unable to function as I normally would. When the suicidal thoughts began to dominate my way of thinking, I felt completely out of control.

During my depression, I began thinking that I was being punished for past mistakes. When my dad was struggling with his depression, I thought that if he would just talk about whatever was bothering him he would get better. He wasn't aware that I knew of the mistakes he had made in the past. A few years before my dad got sick, I learned that he had cheated on my mom. I thought if he would just own his wrongdoings his depression would go away.

My dad never did talk to me about the mistakes he made, and I will never know if he spoke about them with his psychiatrist. However, what I do know is that sharing your darkest secrets and owning your mistakes does not make your depression go away. I know this because I did what I thought my dad couldn't do. I shared my own wrongdoings with the hope that I would be relieved of the burden I was carrying and that I would be released from the darkness I was trapped in.

After what felt like an eternity, but in reality had only been a few months of experiencing postpartum depression, I attempted to "get better" by telling my husband, Chris, that I had had an affair. I explained to him that it took place during the spring of 2001. We were approaching the second anniversary of my dad's death and I was desperate to feel anything other than the pain I felt every time I thought about my dad.

I had met someone who didn't know the me I was before my dad died, he didn't know the sadness that existed in me since my dad died. He only knew me as me and he made me feel incredible. We were friends who spent hours talking about nothing in particular. When I was with him I could laugh without feeling guilty for feeling something other than sadness. I wasn't looking for an affair. I wasn't unhappy in my marriage. I was just unhappy and he managed to make me forget that.

It was more of an emotional affair but an affair none the less. I had crossed a line and I knew it. The affair ended shortly after the anniversary of my dad's death. I realized that this distraction didn't stop me from feeling the emptiness I felt when I thought of my dad. Due to my reckless behavior, I now felt tremendous sadness for the loss of my dad and for the loss of my own values. I knew what I had done was wrong, and I never wanted to make that mistake again. When I ended the affair I made the decision not to tell Chris. I believed I had learned from my mistake and it would be best to shield him from the pain that would come from knowing the details.

Three years later I struggled with the physical and emotional pain of my depression. It impacting my ability to think and function normally. I thought if I could just explain to Chris what I had done, how it happened, and why it happened, then I would be free from my depression. I sat across from him, trembling, trying to find the words to express my regret for the choices I had made. I will never forget the look of devastation in his eyes as I told him. He stayed composed throughout my explanation and then took a few minutes before telling me that he was just as much to blame as I was. He told me I could let go of the guilt I was consumed with and that I didn't need to worry about carrying that burden any further.

My husband handled my confession with poise and grace—everything I needed to be forgiven and yet nothing changed. In fact, my depression worsened. My hope for recovery vanished and it wasn't long before I became suicidal.

While it was not easy to come to the decision to publicly share my mistake, I felt it was necessary in order to properly address the notion that someone struggling with depression brought this upon themselves, or that they can overcome their depression by simply taking responsibility for past mistakes. This is a topic that often comes up in support groups, but there is rarely anyone who can or will adequately address it.

I will share more about my recovery from depression later in the book.

Another theory I would like to address is the idea that depression only affects those who have a family history. There are studies debating whether there is a specific gene causing depression. While I'm not an expert on these studies, through my own experiences and from working with others, it has become clear to me that regardless of family history, depression is often caused by and exacerbated by one or more environmental factors.

These factors include but are not limited to:

- **stress**
     work related
     home related
     relationship related

- **diet**
    too much unhealthy food
    inadequate nutrition
    consumption of foods your body can't easily or
    properly process
- **traumatic events**
- **hormone changes**
- **side effects from medications**
- **lacking adequate physical activity**
- **environmental pollutants**
    toxins in the home
    toxins in the workplace
- **physical and/or emotional abuse**
- **bullying**
- **identity crisis**

In my opinion, family history is not the determining factor for why someone struggles with depression. Though there is a potential benefit that comes from having a family history with depression. It is the same benefit as any other illness. If you are aware of your family history, you might be more proactive about living a healthy lifestyle in an attempt to reduce the chances of being afflicted by depression. You might be more in tune with the symptoms if they should arise, and you might be more capable of getting the necessary help should you need it.

Since losing my dad to suicide I have come to know two things.

1. Suicide is the result of a mental illness.
2. Suicide is not a choice.

Wisdom is nothing more than healed pain.

—Author Unknown

Discussing Suicide with Children

How to talk about suicide with children is a common subject in survivors of suicide support group meetings. People often struggle with what to say and how to say it. Some people feel it is best to hide the truth from children, while others provide every detail. I am of the philosophy that it is best to always be honest with children but only provide age appropriate details.

For example, my daughters were born several years after my dad's death. They have always known that he passed away due to an illness. When my girls were around the ages of five and eight, my older daughter began asking more questions about what type of illness had caused my dad's death. I shared with them that his brain had been sick. I explained to them that he had suffered from depression, and what it meant to have a mental illness. But I continued to limit the details of his actual death.

Roughly four years later, when my daughters were nine and twelve, we had a deeper discussion about depression and suicide. At that time, I explained to them that my dad died from suicide and I answered all of their questions with the utmost honesty. While I have always believed it was important for them to know the truth and to never feel any sense of shame or discomfort from me when I talk about my dad's death, I also felt that there was no reason to burden them with the details at an age when they couldn't properly process the information. My intention was to openly discuss my dad's death with them once I felt they had the ability to properly understand mental illness and the impact mental illness can have on a person.

On the day of my dad's death, my nephew and two nieces were at the house. Cole was just about to turn five, Marissa was four, and Makayla was two. It is my understanding that while they spent much of the day fully aware that something terrible took place, they were completely unaware of what had actually happened. After I arrived at my mom's house, I quickly realized their uncertainty of the situation. Cole and Makayla's mom was consumed with grief and Marissa's mom was flying back from California. Chris and I decided to remove the three children from the house even if it was just for a little break.

I will always remember their solemn faces as we drove away from my mom's house. Each one of them had a look of sadness mixed with fear and yet it was clear from our initial conversation with them that they did not know what had happened to their grandpa. No one had known what to tell them; how do you explain suicide to someone so young?

Chris and I decided that what they needed more than anything was to have some fun and not be burdened with the details just yet. We took them to an indoor play area where they could temporarily forget all the panic and distress they had witnessed earlier in the day. I look back on that decision and realize what a blessing it was for me to have that time focused on the kids, on their laughter, and on their excitement. For a brief time, my energy wasn't consumed by questions and sadness.

After our play time had come to an end, we began our return to my mom's house. As we drove, we spoke with the kids about what they had seen and heard that morning. When we arrived, I turned to them to see Makayla sleeping peacefully, but Cole and Marissa both had concerned looks on their faces. With a great deal of sadness, I told them their grandpa had died. I explained to them that his brain had been sick. They asked if anyone else would get sick and die, too. I tried my best to help them understand that this wasn't like a cold or flu and that no one else would "catch" it.

Discussing Suicide with Children

In October of 2016, I sent Marissa a digital copy of what I thought was my final version of this book. It wasn't until then that I realized how little anyone had spoken with her about my dad's death. Within hours of emailing her a copy, I received several text messages from her. The love and support she expressed for what I had written was more than I could have asked for. As I continued to read her messages I was saddened to learn that she had never really known the details of what happened, and had not wanted to upset anyone by asking questions. In that moment, I realized I needed to add a section to this book regarding how and when to talk to children about suicide.

Over the years, I've heard many people share their struggles with how to talk to children, but there is one story that will always hold a special place in my heart. I was attending a meeting where a woman spoke of losing her son-in-law to suicide. She was concerned her daughter was not coping well and that her granddaughter, who was seven at the time, wasn't being told the truth about what happened to her dad. As the days and months passed, her concerns grew stronger so she began to research how to best talk to children about suicide and came across an article she thought was perfect.

After discussing her concerns with her daughter, she received permission to have an open conversation with her granddaughter. She planned a special day for her and her granddaughter that revolved around things her son-in-law had enjoyed. They spent the day talking about him and reminiscing about what they remembered and loved most about him.

At the end of the day, she told her granddaughter that she wanted to talk to her about how her dad had died. She explained to her that he died from a brain attack which caused his brain to stop functioning normally. She went on to tell her granddaughter that it is similar to when someone has a heart attack resulting in their heart malfunctioning and causing them to die.

She told our group that her granddaughter quietly cried for several minutes and then said, "So it wasn't my fault that he died and that mom is so upset?" The woman shared with that at that moment she realized the burden her granddaughter had been carrying. She hugged her tightly and did her best to assure her that none of it was her fault. She then continued to answer other questions her granddaughter had.

Regardless of how you choose to explain suicide to a child, what is important is that you are honest and open in your discussions. Encourage them to talk about their loved one and to ask questions. Help them to know that whatever emotion they are feeling is normal and part of the grieving process. If you have children and you feel you are incapable of openly discussing suicide, please find a friend or relative who can play that role for you. Do everything you can to help your children understand why you are unable to discuss this loss and that your inability to discuss it should not stop them from talking with others. Children need to know they have someone they can openly and honestly talk to about their loved one and about suicide.

It is common for a child to take on the blame for why a bad situation occurred. Children, even more than adults, need to be reassured that the suicide was a result of an illness and not anything the child did or didn't do. This is not a one-time conversation that will never be questioned again. Be prepared to answer questions as they come up and be willing to be vulnerable and honest in your answers. It has been my experience that this will build trust and understanding in your relationship.

Exercise 6: Create a "Stories of My Loved One" Book

Collaborate with friends and family to create a book of short stories about the person you lost. This is especially beneficial to children and/or grandchildren of the person who passed away. Ask friends and family members to contribute to the project by simply sending out an email to various people asking them to include the following information:

- When did you first meet . . . ?
- How would you best describe your relationship with . . . ?
- Please share your favorite story of . . . ?

The greatest healing therapy is Love.

—Hubert H. Humphrey

What If & If Only

The "What Ifs" and "If Onlys" can be easy to think about.

> "What if I had gotten home 10 minutes earlier?"
> "If only I had realized he was that sick."
> "If only I had done more."
> "What if he were still alive today?"
> "Things would be so much better if only he were still here."

Thoughts and statements that consist of "what if" or "if only" can be a natural and yet very dangerous way of thinking. These thoughts and statements are an easy trap to fall into and will prevent you from truly moving forward and healing. It is important that you challenge yourself to focus on the here and now and not get stuck on what could have been. One of the most empowering tools for healthy healing is to acknowledge, in order to move forward, you must let go of the "what ifs."

Over the years, I have heard people discuss how they had no idea that their loved one was depressed. They wondered how this could happen when they didn't even know there was a struggle. Others have talked about how hard it was to watch their loved one struggle day after day with their depression. They shared how hopeless they felt and yet, wondered if they could have done more.

Some people have talked about the fight they had just experienced with their loved one or the fight that recently took place between their loved one and another person. There is often someone who shares how their loved one had recently lost their job or had some other difficult hardship develop. Each of these survivors expressed their frustration in wondering if they could have prevented this tragedy from happening if they had just been more compassionate and less critical. They described their anger and the blame they felt for the person or situation that appeared to be the trigger for the suicide.

I have witnessed people become paralyzed by the "what ifs"; consumed not only by the pain of their loss but also by the fear they might lose another loved one to suicide. They are terrified they didn't do enough for their loved one or they made a mistake in how they handled the situation. They begin making decisions based out of fear of losing another loved one to suicide which often result in unhealthy and dysfunctional relationships. Fear based decision-making tends to be irrational and detrimental to everyone involved.

It is common for survivors of suicide to feel guilty following the death of their loved one. It can take time for survivors to truly believe that they are not responsible for this loss. A big fight, unkind words, expressing frustration, or having a lack of sympathy for your loved one's depression didn't cause the suicide. Suicide doesn't occur after those types of encounters when the person is healthy. Recognizing your loved one suffered from an illness that impacted their ability to make rational decisions is the key to letting go of any guilt or blame you might be holding on to.

Knowing the rate of suicide is higher for those who have been intimately affected by it means that, as survivors, we should be prepared for how to handle the situation if another loved one is struggling with depression.

Helping others through their depression doesn't mean you bear the burden of making sure they recover. It simply means you are patient and supportive in their time of need. Help them by researching and accessing available treatment options. The most important aspect in helping others is to care for them in a manner that is healthy for both of you. Support them to the best of your ability without judgment or blame, but with the understanding you are not responsible for their recovery.

Treat your loved one with respect by communicating that you understand their struggle is not a choice. Help them to feel loved and supported by acknowledging depression is an illness. As they go through the ups and downs of recovery, be there for them in ways that shows you're committed to helping them return to a healthy state of mind. You can do this by offering to help them with various tasks or commitments your loved one is juggling.

Some people have the best intentions when helping a loved one, but can do more damage than good if they don't truly understand the difference between enabling someone and empowering them. To enable someone is to show love and kindness, but in ways which allow the person to stay stagnant in their development or to deteriorate. To empower someone is to show love and kindness through methods in which the person is challenged to grow in a supportive environment. Truly helping someone involves assisting them in developing healthy habits and discovering tools to success rather than doing things for them. Empowerment builds confidence and increases self-esteem.

It is important to stay focused on your objective, which is to help your loved one overcome their depression and, in doing this, it is imperative you avoid critical or judgmental comments. All of the people I have spoken to about their struggles with depression have had one thing in common–they felt guilty and/or ashamed for being sick.

Exercise 7: Moving Past "What If"

On a piece of paper make your own list of "what ifs" and "if onlys." Write them all down. Read them over. Make sure the list is as complete as possible. Now take the list and tear it up, burn it, do whatever is necessary to destroy it.

This list consumes too much of your heart and mind. Let it go! Focus on how you can move forward in a way that honors you and the person you lost.

For instance, I still think about how my dad would have handled situations I'm currently facing. Growing up I respected him, and I believed in the advice he would give me. Since his death, I have faced various difficult situations, and I have often taken a moment to reflect on lessons I learned from him. I have also stopped what I was doing to talk to him; to ask him what he would do in my situation. I then allow myself time to process my thoughts and emotions before I move forward. I would like to believe this way of reflecting on who he was before he got sick helps me to stay in tune with him without being fixated on wishing he was still here.

Accept what IS, let go of what WAS, and have faith in what will BE.

—Sonia Ricotti

Anger

Anger is a common emotion often associated with losing someone to suicide. Anger can be one of the biggest reasons we struggle with healing. For some people, they are angry at the person they lost; for others, they are angry at the lack of support from doctors; some are angry at themselves; while others are angry at God. And for many, they are angry at everyone and everything. They are so overwhelmed by the magnitude of pain, shock, and sadness they don't even know where to direct their anger.

I was never angry at my dad. I never once blamed him for what happened. If anything, I often felt that I, along with his doctors, had let him down. My heart was broken at the thought of how much he must have been suffering. How did I not know and why didn't he tell me. Or did he try, and I wasn't able to hear what he was saying?

Those questions fueled my anger at myself. For years I worked with various support groups and therapists in an effort to work through my anger and to realize I was not at fault. I could not hold myself responsible for not doing more to help him. It wasn't until I was working at a crisis center that I met a man who would forever change my view on my dad's death. Until meeting this man, I was often consumed by sadness and anger at myself when I thought about my dad.

While working at a Bay Area crisis center, one of our volunteers told me his own story about how he had attempted suicide. He had sailed his boat out to dangerous waters during a storm with the expectation that if the storm didn't sink his boat, the rocks in the surrounding area would. Amazingly he survived both the storm and the rocks. He and his boat were discovered after the storm passed. He shared with me how angry he was that he had survived. Over time he began to question if maybe the reason he survived was for a greater purpose. He was hoping volunteering at the crisis center might provide him with some clarity.

His words will remain with me. "I'm alive but I'm not really living. My body is here and I'm going through the motions but I don't feel anything but pain. All I want to do is die and yet here I am. I hurt all day, and when I'm not hurting, I don't feel anything at all. I have promised my children I will get better but I don't even know if that is possible. I really believe the only way for me to find any peace is to leave this life and go on to the next."

I listened to this man. I pictured his children and, for a moment, I was jealous of how lucky they were he was trying to survive for them. But the more I looked at him and listened to his story, the more I realized how much pain he was in; a pain that no words could adequately describe.

I thought of my own dad, the way he looked before he died. This man's body language reminded of how it felt to hug my dad the last time I saw him. I could remember feeling my dad's arms around me, hugging me and yet it felt so unfamiliar. It was like hugging a hollow shell of a person I didn't know.

As I listened to this man speak with no emotion in his voice, I continued to be reminded of what it was like to be with my dad before he died. I watched this man as he spoke and realized it was his eyes that most reminded me of my dad . . . they were so empty.

While his story was both sad and heartfelt, his eyes were lifeless. I didn't see any sign of excitement that would express that he had been saved for a bright future. I didn't see sadness or despair. I saw nothing. It was then that I allowed myself to believe my dad was in a better place. I realized even if he were still alive, he wouldn't be living.

After that conversation, I knew in my heart that my dad had reached a point in his depression in which he had become terminal, and it wouldn't have mattered what I did or didn't do. It was time for him to move on. With this, I realized I needed to forgive myself so I could move on too.

I learned that truly letting go of my anger required me to first find the strength to forgive.

We do not heal the past by dwelling there; we heal the past by living fully in the present.

—Marianne Williamson

Forgiveness

Forgiveness—such a simple word and yet such a difficult action. Why is forgiveness so hard?

At one point or another, we've all been in a situation where we've been hurt. Whether we were hurt by someone else or we managed to hurt ourselves, the result is the same—we have to find a way to forgive in order to move forward in a healthy manner.

For many, forgiveness is difficult because they believe by forgiving someone they are admitting defeat. But in reality it is quite the opposite. Being able to forgive someone requires strength. It requires a sense of compassion and a willingness to understand and be free of judgment. Forgiveness isn't about who's right or wrong. It's about letting go of any negativity that has the potential to consume the person holding onto it.

Forgiveness is challenging for most of us. We as a culture are not taught how to forgive. We often hear that old adage, "forgive and forget." But I believe it should really be, "forgive and learn." We should never forget—but in order to move forward we must learn. We must have the willingness to learn from difficult situations.

Forgiving someone provides you closure to a difficult situation. That doesn't mean you need to have an ongoing relationship with the person who hurt you. You will need to determine your own wellbeing and what type of relationship you are capable of maintaining. Sometimes we have to love people from a distance in order to maintain a healthy way of life.

Our willingness to forgive others and ourselves, while incredibly difficult, is also critical to our overall health and wellbeing. Forgiveness allows us the opportunity to let go, move forward, and be at peace. So, how does one forgive?

I have read a few books on forgiveness. What I discovered was I needed someone to teach me how to forgive the author for wasting my time and money on a book that talked about the importance of forgiving, but left me feeling inept at how to actually do it. Ultimately, there have been two events in my life which have helped me learn how to truly forgive. The first was having children, and the second was rediscovering my relationship with God.

If I was going to come up with a "How to Forgive" guide, it would be short and simple. I have come to believe that learning to forgive is a daily 4-step process.

1. The ability to forgive starts by practicing forgiveness for even the smallest of things on a daily basis. When someone says, "I'm sorry," respond with, "I forgive you," instead of saying the usual, "That's fine," or "No big deal." This sounds simple but it can be hard to do when someone has just smashed your hand in a door and all you want to do is scream at them. Practice saying the words, "I forgive you," and try to genuinely mean it.

2. Have an open mind and an open heart. Be willing to understand another perspective. Allowing someone else to have a different point of view doesn't make them right, it makes them human. Each of us has our own interpretation of the events that take place on any given day. To be understanding and willing to have differences allows you to be a better friend, sibling, parent, child, etc.

3. Focus on the positive aspects of your life and smile as much as possible. Look around—this is a pretty amazing world we live in with lots of things to make us smile. I have found that being outside and just simply looking into the sky can bring a smile to my face. Look for things throughout your day that can make you feel happy or relaxed. You may be surprised by how

many simple things throughout your day brighten your mood once you start looking for them.

4. Say a prayer. Talk to God. Ask Him to give you the strength to forgive, especially when forgiveness feels like an impossible task. If you truly want to let go of your negative feelings toward another person and move forward, ask God to help you forgive and to fill your heart with love—even if you can only love them from a distance. Ask God to help each of you to make better choices and to be filled with love.

This is a time of humility and a time to recognize that we all make mistakes; so also ask God to forgive you for the mistakes you've made. Ask Him to help those who you've hurt to find it in their hearts to forgive you. And finally, ask God to help you learn and grow from your struggles in order recognize the blessings you face as you move forward.

Exercise 8: Commit to Forgiveness

1. Say the words, "I forgive you," the next time someone apologizes to you.
2. Be willing to hear someone else's point of view and allow yourself time to process it before you respond.
3. Find time in your day to recognize something that brings a smile to your face—now enjoy that moment.
4. Make an effort to ask God in assisting you in letting go of any hard feelings that you might be holding on to.

Forgive others, not because they deserve
forgiveness, but because you deserve peace.

—Author Unknown

Where Was God?

The day my dad died so did my relationship with God. It wasn't intentional; I just simply stopped praying, stopped believing, and stopped asking Him for help. I wasn't consciously aware that I was angry with Him or that I blamed Him for what happened. It was more that I simply shut down and could no longer talk to Him. It was too painful to ask Him for help. It felt like a betrayal to my dad to even think about asking God for help, given that I was questioning why He hadn't been there to help my dad. So in moments of weakness, I found myself talking to my dad about situations and asking him for guidance.

Nearly eleven years after my dad died, I met three special people who helped me to see that while I was talking to my dad, I was also praying to my Heavenly Father. Previous to this realization, when asked how I had managed to heal so well after losing my dad, I would respond by saying, "I was very lucky to have the right people in my life at the right time."

It was my dear friend and holistic chiropractor, Dr. H., who helped me to see that luck had nothing to do with it. He encouraged me to open my heart and to let go of my own constraints in order for me to see it was God who had brought those people to me. My initial reaction to this idea was a mixture of fear and guilt. I have five siblings and a mom who all survived the same painful experience of losing my dad, and yet very few of them have moved forward in a healthy and constructive way. So I asked Dr. H. the question that was causing me so much angst at the idea of believing I had been blessed, "Why would God bless me with the love and support that I have received and not provide the same blessings to the rest of my family?"

With love in his eyes and tenderness in his voice, Dr. H. responded with, "Ah, Jenny, it's not that he only chose to bless you with these opportunities—it is that you were open to receiving these blessings. You accepted the love and support, including the hard work that came with them."

While I heard his words, it took some time for the message to sink in. This wasn't an easy concept to believe but with some soul searching, reflection, and much "discussion" with my dad, I began to know it to be true. I had been presented with people who helped me to heal and to find peace within myself. With each one of those interactions came a struggle; a struggle from which I often wanted to walk away. Each person who helped me required a commitment from me. They asked for complete honesty from me; and most of all, they forced me to truly feel the pain that was consuming me. They helped me realize the only way to let go of my pain was to allow myself to feel it completely.

When I look back at these moments, I realize the pain was nearly unbearable at times, but I not only survived the pain, I became stronger for having gone through it. One of the most challenging yet rewarding experiences for me was accepting God back in my life. It required me to humble myself and to realize that I had been holding on to anger directed at the One who had been trying to save me.

This moment required me to forgive and to ask for forgiveness. I realized I had to let go of the anger and sadness I once thought was protecting me from being disappointed by Him again. I also had to ask Him to forgive me for not realizing He had been with me all this time. I began to understand that He had been there wrapping me in His arms and protecting me with His love through all the moments when I thought I had been alone and broken. And it was then that I slowly and awkwardly said my first official prayer. When I finished praying, I was filled with an indescribable sense of peace and even more love for my dad and my Father in Heaven.

Where Was God?

My connection to and awareness of God was restored through saying my first prayer since my dad died. It took place on June 2, 2010, on the eleventh anniversary of my dad's death. I hadn't planned it to happen that way, but I have to wonder if maybe He had.

Even after my first prayer, I still struggled with how to have a relationship with God. I felt more at peace after I welcomed prayer back into my life, but I didn't feel complete; in fact, I kind of felt like a phony. I couldn't put my finger on why I felt this way, but I knew I was missing something. When I would talk about this feeling with my friends, they would say, "You just need to put God first."

Over and over again, I would hear or read this phrase, *Put God First*. But what did that mean? How do I put Him first? Out of fear of looking stupid, I never asked my friends what it meant to put God first. But one day in 2013 while living in Memphis, I was working with a woman who practiced energy healing through the use of fork tuning. We were discussing the struggles I was facing at that time and she said, "You have to put God first and everything else will fall into place."

I tried to hold back my tears, but I couldn't any longer. How was everything going to fall into place if I didn't know how to put God first? I found the courage to finally ask the question I had been too afraid to ask over the last couple of years.

Her answer was simple, "When you wake up in the morning and before you go to sleep at night, thank Him. Before you begin your day's activities, ask Him to be with you. Before you speak or take action, ask for His guidance. In essence, recognize that He is with you at all times and He will guide you if you're willing to listen."

How could such a simple answer have caused me two years of heartache? I had spent all this time looking for some huge gesture I thought I was supposed to be doing to try to match what God was doing for me. The reality is that all He asks of us is to look for Him throughout our day, to share His love with those around us, and to ask Him to guide us in our actions. What is truly remarkable about God is that He will do all those things and more even if we don't ask. But we can't feel the true benefits of His blessings until we recognize that His love and strength surround us at all times.

So, where was God? He was and always is with each and every one of us. We just have to open our hearts to see Him. Some might ask where God was when my dad needed him most. My heart tells me God was right there through it all. He surrounded my dad with His love and welcomed him home where he could now be free of his earthly pain and feel the ultimate peace of being in the arms of God.

I sometimes look back and laugh at the idea that it took me moving to Las Vegas to reconnect with God. You never know where God will make Himself known to you. I feel incredibly blessed to have moved to Las Vegas in 2009; where I was fortunate to meet people who would push me out of my comfort zone, and who would be willing to take a chance on me by sharing their own love of God with me.

Be joyful in hope, patient in affliction, faithful in prayer.

—Romans 12:12

Remembering the Person You Lost

It might seem impossible to forget who your loved one was to you. Over time even precious memories can begin to fade. Take the time to write down what you remember about your loved one. The funny things they were known to say, what they did that made you laugh, or the things about them that annoyed you. Write them down because over time memories will fade; even the things you once thought would be impossible to forget.

I recently found a book in which I had written memories of my dad. I smiled at what I had written and was surprised how much I had forgotten.

Things I want to remember about my dad . . .

- He used to always say, "You should never put anything in your ear smaller than your elbow." Later he would use his pocket knife to scratch or clean out the inside of his ear.
- While driving on road trips if anyone was getting too rowdy or if there was fighting between any of us, he was notorious for saying, "Don't make me pull over this car."
- He didn't have to yell to make his point. But he would jab his index finger into the soft spot just below your shoulder when he felt he needed to be clear about the message he was sending.
- He would often pause in thought about what he was about to say when it was something serious or if it was a delicate subject.
- He always stopped to help people in need. On road trips or just driving around town; if he saw someone in trouble, he would pull over and offer his assistance.

- He made a wooden paddle when he realized that using his belt as punishment (mostly on my older brother) was actually damaging his belt. We called his paddle Dad's Doomer. He later made another one that we called Mom's Mercy.

- He would eat a bowl of cereal as he drove to work while driving a stick shift. He would steer the car with his knees.

- WhataBurger—My dad worked shift work at a local power plant. The night before he would switch to working the midnight shift, he would stay up all night watching movies. When I was 10 he started letting me stay up with him. I would always fall asleep. But when he started to feel like he was going to fall asleep, he would wake me up and tell me it was time to go. We would then sneak out of the house and drive to WhataBurger to get a late night/early morning snack.

- One day when I was in high school, I complained about the bathroom being cold in the mornings. Without me asking, he started turning on the bathroom heater before he left for work. It was a small act of kindness, but a huge gesture of love.

Exercise 9: Memories

Buy a journal and take the time to write down the memories you want to remember about your loved one. In addition to keeping track of your memories, consider documenting any dreams you might have following your loved one's death. It is easy to think these dreams might feel too strong to ever forget; but like any other memory, these, too, will fade.

Trauma creates change you DON'T choose.
Healing is about creating change you DO choose.

—Michelle Rosenthall

The Lessons I've Learned

There are three very important lessons I've learned while going through my own grieving process. The first is not all blessings feel like a blessing at the time. The second is healing is greatly impacted by your mindset and intention. The third lesson is you are truly a product of the people you choose to surround you.

Lesson 1

Over the last 17 years, I have had the task of recovering from losing my dad to suicide. It has been full of both dreadful and beautiful moments. I am in a position now to look back at my journey and recognize the blessings that came from such tragedy. I have realized it is easy to take small blessings for granted on a daily basis, and we don't always recognize a blessing until we've had time to look back on it.

For example, during the fall of 1999, within six months after losing my dad, I had the opportunity to participate in a specialized eight-week process group specifically for people who had lost a loved one to suicide. In order for me to participate in this group I had to commit to being present for each of the eight classes. During these eight weeks, I began to dread Wednesdays because our meetings could be painfully intense.

My drive there was filled with anxiety over what would be discussed that night and what emotions would arise. I would leave feeling drained, exhausted, and sometimes defeated. Not only was I processing my own grief, I was intimately affected by the grief of the other seven participants. It was a process that would leave a lasting mark on me; and ultimately be a part of the reason I'm determined to help other people.

After completing the eight-week program, participants could attend a monthly support group organized by the facilitator of the process group. It wasn't until 2004 that I attended a "typical" survivor of suicide support group, and I was extremely disappointed by the experience. The group was led by a woman who had lost her fiancé 20 years prior. Her emotion was still so raw that she allowed her own feelings to be pushed onto what others were saying and feeling.

It was after attending a few meetings like this that I realized how fortunate I had been to experience the eight-week process group so soon after my dad died. While it had been exceptionally difficult to go through the eight weeks, I had been given much needed tools to heal. The program helped me to understand that I wasn't alone in my grief, and it gave me a safe place to express myself while fully processing my loss. I had been blessed in ways I didn't even realize until I was faced with the reality of what most people experience while dealing with the loss of a loved one to suicide.

Another blessing that took me years to recognize was my dad's death. Perceiving his death as a blessing is a result of the fact that I believe his suicide ultimately saved my life. In September 1999, while living in San Francisco, I was introduced to acupuncture as a treatment option for panic attacks from which I had begun to suffer as a result of my dad's death. I was fortunate to work with an incredible acupuncturist who helped me to see alternative healing methods and Eastern medicine in a whole new light. As a result, I would continue to benefit from this form of healing therapy throughout my life.

In February 2003, my husband and I moved to Minnesota where later that year I gave birth to a beautiful baby girl. It was a difficult pregnancy with a complicated delivery, and a challenging start to parenthood with very little support as we were still new to the area. Shortly after giving birth, I began suffering from postpartum depression.

Within a few months, I started having suicidal thoughts. It was like I had two brains: the rational slow moving one, while the second one moved at rapid speed and never stopped. The rational brain would think, "You have to take care of your baby. You need to make dinner. You need to take a shower." While the other brain would think, "You're going to die! You could use that razor. You could take those pills. You could drive off the bridge." I couldn't make the second brain turn off—it was a constant flow of unwanted thoughts that were getting louder every day. I felt out of control and terrified, not just for myself but for the safety of our daughter.

I had previously been a crisis counselor and should have known how to get help. However, during that time I was so sick I didn't know what to do or who to talk to. I was struggling to function on a basic level. Knowing what my dad had experienced while taking antidepressants, I knew I didn't want to take medication.

I was scared and I didn't know how to describe what I was experiencing; but I knew I was going to die if I didn't get help. It **was not** easy. But one day as soon as my husband came home from work, I said the words out loud, "I'm scared I'm going to die."

Until that point, we had not even discussed the fact that I was struggling with depression. I will never forget the look of concern in his eyes as he walked toward me. Without any hesitation, he said, "Let's get you back in acupuncture. I'll come home to be with the baby so you can get the help you need."

I truly believe if it had not been for my dad's death, my husband would not have taken my concerns seriously; and if I had not been introduced to acupuncture after his death, we would not have known to use it as a means of treatment for my own depression. Acupuncture was not an immediate fix—there is no immediate fix to depression. It took me several months of weekly acupuncture. But eventually it did relieve me of my depression and return me to a happy, fully functioning wife and mom.

Three years after delivering my first daughter, I continued to receive acupuncture through my second pregnancy. I can say with relief, I didn't experience a single day of postpartum depression.

While I felt grateful for having managed my depression through the use of acupuncture, I still hadn't fully realized the blessing it was in my life until several years later. During January of 2013, a friend of a friend wrote a suicide note and posted it on Facebook. He then disappeared for nearly two days before he was found and taken to get the help he needed. During those two days, I felt overwhelming concern for this man, his wife, and their young children. I followed the updates closely and I even posted a message of love and support on his Facebook page.

On the day of his disappearance, I remember driving to pick up my children from school, I found myself consumed by how this man's family must be feeling. I felt desperate in my hope for someone to find him and help him. It was then that I realized how my own depression could have taken my life and left my daughter without her mother and my husband without his wife. I thought about how acupuncture saved my life and how I had only discovered acupuncture as a way to cope with losing my dad. In that moment I was flooded with gratitude for my dad; fully recognizing that his death had saved my life.

Lesson 2

Some might say it is selfish for me to think of my dad's death as a blessing—and even more selfish to think that he died in order to save me. I, too, have had moments when I belived it was selfish to have such thoughts. I have rarely spoken to my family about my dad's death due to my feelings of guilt over the fact that I'm not only at peace with his death, but I'm grateful to him for his death. The reality of my situation is, from the time my dad died, it was incredibly important to me that I find a way for his death to be a positive force in my life.

The Lessons I've Learned

Working on this project compelled me to revisit old journals and letters. It pushed me out of my comfort zone and required me to speak to my siblings about a time that we rarely speak of. It opened my eyes to see how important one's mindset is when it comes to healing. Those who want peace, who want to grow, who want to find something positive in an otherwise negative situation **will** find what they are looking for. It is important to keep in mind that often the answers we're looking for require patience and a willingness to wait for the right moment before we can discover them.

I also believe that healing is greatly impacted by our intentions and our willingness to allow good things to happen. For everyone in my family, June 2nd will forever be the day that changed our lives. It was the day we all realized how sick our dad was and that none of us were able to help him.

For the first few years, I dreaded the anniversary of his death. The second year was the hardest for me. The anticipation leading up to the anniversary was unnerving. I became wreckless in an attempt to feel anything other than the intense loss and pain that came from thinking of my dad.

I made upsetting decisions which damaged friendships and could have ruined my marriage. I acted like a fool, and the sad part is it didn't even work. June 2nd still came and I still felt the sadness I had desperatly tried to avoid. But I learned two things. One, the anticipation of the anniversary is far more painful than the day itself. I can't really explain why but it's almost a relief by the time the actual day arrives. Two, I realized I didn't want June 2nd to be a day of unbearable sadness, but I didn't want it to be just another day either. In my heart I secretly wished for June 2nd to be a day of great opportunity.

On the fourth anniversary of my dad's death, I got my wish . . . **June 2, 2003,** was the day Chris and I saw our baby's first heartbeat. On the eleventh anniversary, my wish came true again . . . **June 2, 2010,** was the day our older daughter graduated from Kindergarten and the day I reconnected to God. On the fifteenth anniversary . . . **June 2, 2014,** was the first day of farm camp for my daughters. It is their favorite place to spend the day and I'm grateful to be in a position where I can truly be happy for their excitement over a new adventure. On the sixteenth anniversary . . . **June 2, 2015,** was the day Chris and I entered into a contract to purchase what we plan to be our forever home in Minnesota.

June 2nd will always be a day for me to reflect on the love I shared with my dad. I might cry as I think about all the times we had together and all he did for me as I grew up. I will always thank him for everything he went through, and the sacrifice he made for me to live my life to its fullest potential. I will focus my energy and intention on making the most out of whatever that day brings me.

Lesson 3

I've become aware that to achieve healthy healing, it is critial for you to not only surround yourself with people who will inspire you, who will challenge you, who will add to your overall well-being; but it is equally as important to remove the people who are unhealthy and are draining you.

It has taken me several years and a great deal of heartache to fully realize the importance of the last part of that statement. The truth is that no matter how many good people you are around, you will only be as good and as healthy as the least healthy person in your circle. Letting go of people can be painful. If you're letting go with the intention of bettering yourself, then remember that you can still love that person . . . just love them from a distance.

I have recently had to do just that. I have had to tell someone I love that I can no longer interact with them. I desperately wanted to make my relationship with this person a healthy one, but I discovered that it was only causing me anxiety, frustration, and disappointment. I was then allowing the relationship to impact my own behavior with others. I realized this was no way to live and it was not how I wanted my daughters to experience me. Telling this person goodbye was a difficult decision but it's one I'm at peace with.

Within days of taking action to remove this unhealthy person from my life, I was asked by a dear friend to work on a project that could possibly help her two friends, who were struggling with their own losses of loved ones to suicide. I felt honored to be asked and, for the first time, I felt capable of doing it. For years I have wanted to help others but I haven't known how. Every time I would start working on an idea, it would slip away. It's as if I wasn't ready yet; and now that my heart is free and my conscience is clear, I'm able to share my experiences with the hope that I can be a positive force for someone else.

*You cannot get through a single day without
having an impact on the world around you.
What you do makes a difference, and you
have to decide what kind of difference you
want to make.*

—Jane Gooddall

The Bond

While there is a bond connecting all survivors of suicide, it is important to remember each survivor has their own journey, their own path to healing. I encourage connecting with other survivors of suicide and being open to learning from their experiences. Each one of us has been impacted in a way that those who have never been touched by suicide will never understand, will never be able to relate to, and can make the healing process feel that much more daunting when trying to face it alone.

I believe a vital aspect of my healing has been from sharing my journey with other survivors. That is why I encourage all survivors to attend healthy support groups as often as needed for an indefinite amount of time. As I have mentioned, it has been over seventeen years since I lost my dad, and I still find comfort in attending a good support group. It is a safe place where you can freely discuss your loved one and any feelings or emotions that you are experiencing without fearing judgment from others.

It is important we talk about our loved ones, openly discuss their illness, and work together to tear down the stigma associated with depression and suicide. My ultimate goal, and why I chose to share my experience, has been driven by my desire to find something good in what could have otherwise been viewed as an unnecessary tragedy.

We all have a story to share; we all have the opportunity to make a difference. Maybe we couldn't save the person we lost, but maybe that was so we could help someone else. Each one of us has the ability to come together in support of one another, to support those struggling with depression, and to support the movement to change how we as a society view those struggling with depression. It is up to us to break down the stigma associated with suicide.

My hope is that one day we can all feel at peace with the loss we have experienced. While sadness may come and go, the peace in knowing that our loved one died from an illness and is no longer in pain is a peace that provides a constant source of comfort even during our saddest moments.

Much love to you all.

Healing doesn't mean the damage never existed. It means the damage no longer controls our lives.

—Akshay Dubey

Don't Quit

When things go wrong, as they sometimes will,
When the road you're trudging seems all uphill,
When funds are low and the debts are high,
And you want to smile but you have to sigh,
When care is pressing you down a bit,
Rest if you must, but don't you quit.
Life is queer with its twists and turns,
As every one of us sometimes learns,
And many a failure turns about,
When he might have won if he'd stuck it out.
Don't give up, though the pace seems slow -
You may succeed with another blow.
Often the goal is nearer than
It seems to a faint and faltering man;
Often the struggler has given up
When he might have captured the victor's cup,
And he learned too late, when the night slipped down,
How close he was to the golden crown.
Success is failure turned inside out -
The silver tint of the clouds of doubt,
And you never can tell how close you are -
It may be near when it seems afar;
So stick to the fight when you're hardest hit -
It's when things seem worst that you mustn't quit.

—Author Unknown

Thank you

I have been truly blessed by the love of my friends and family. To all of you who supported me, believed in me and pushed me to be more and to do more than I ever thought I could, thank you.

Amy, Tara, & Dr. Hetzel—Thank you for helping me to reconnect with God and for helping me realize that I was blessed and not just lucky. Who would have guessed that moving to Las Vegas would help me to discover my faith?

Amy—I cannot imagine my life without your infectious smile and positive energy. You are always up for anything and willing to offer everything to help a friend.

Tara—Thank you for being the spark that helped me see this project come to life. You have taught me a great deal about healthy healing and what it means to be truly healthy and not just going through the motions.
I am truly grateful to each of you for your friendship and your continued love and support.

Barbara and Keith—Thank you for helping me to take my faith to a deeper level. I am grateful to you for always being there to listen and offer words of encouragement in my times of need. Your continuous love and support have been a tremendous blessing to me and my family.

Kellie—Thank you for loving me and not giving up on me when I was miserable and probably unworthy of your love. You taught me patience, kindness, and that I don't always have to say everything I'm thinking. You stood up for me and defended me when no one else understood my struggle. I will forever be grateful for your friendship and for all you continue to do to stay connected.

Kendra—From our first conversation I have believed that we must have been connected in another life. I am truly grateful to you for all of your love and support. You have been a tremendous friend providing me with guidance when I've felt lost. Thank you for being you and for sharing who you are with me.

Dana & Judy—Words cannot describe the impact that you have had in my life thanks to your unconditional love and support. I am blessed to call you my family and that my daughters think of you as grandparents. Thank you for everything you have done for me. I love you.

Mary Ellen—You have been my best friend for as long as I can remember. You know me better than anyone and you have continued to love me even when you didn't like my choices. I'm grateful for your honesty and for your ability to challenge me while still making me feel loved. Thank you for always being there for me and for giving me strength when I've been weak.

Chris—When we first met I thought that if I pretended to be the person you wanted me to be, then you would fall in love with me, and sure enough you asked me to marry you. For years I feared that one day you would figure out that I was a fraud, and then recently I realized that at first I might have been pretending to be who you wanted, but in reality you had helped me to become who I wanted to be. Thank you for challenging me and for loving me. Most of all thank you for not giving up on me and not allowing me to give up on us.

Thank You

Kaeli and Grace—I dedicate this book to you. I hope that you will always know who your Papa Scott was to me and how much I loved him. I hope this book provides you with a clear understanding of his illness and his death. Above all, I hope you understand that your greatest struggles can become your greatest blessings. It is up to you to find the good in every situation.

I don't have the words to convey to you how much you have helped me to be a better person but I want you both to know that being your mom has brought out the best in who I am and what I have to offer this world. Thank you for loving me, for continuously teaching me new things, and for believing in me. I feel incredibly blessed to be your mom.

Online Resources

www.suicide.org

www.afsp.org

www.allianceofhope.org

www.save.org

www.projectsemicolon.com

www.growingoutofdarkness.org

Made in the USA
Columbia, SC
20 June 2021